Latin American Theology:
Radical or Evangelical?

Latin American Theology
Radical or Evangelical?
The Struggle for the Faith in a Young Church

by
C. PETER WAGNER
Associate General Director
Andes Evangelical Mission

WILLIAM B. EERDMANS PUBLISHING COMPANY
GRAND RAPIDS, MICHIGAN

Affectionately dedicated to
one of the twentieth-century's distinguished prophets
DONALD A. McGAVRAN
and his colleagues on the faculty of the
Fuller Theological Seminary
School of World Mission and Institute of Church Growth

22779

CONTENTS

INTRODUCTION

A new theological debate has recently been taking shape in Latin American Protestantism. It is new at least to Latin America, for a debate on similar issues has been raging for some years now in the traditionally Protestant countries. In contrast to the now outmoded, anti-Catholic polemics that were directed to those outside the Protestant church in Latin America, this new debate is pitting Protestant against Protestant. The heart of the matter concerns the mission of the church in the world.

Not that the debate is confined to Protestants. Virtually identical sides are being chosen within the Roman Catholic Church. As a matter of fact, one large segment of aggiornamento-minded Catholics engaged in the struggle for renewal in their own church are more closely identified theologically with the radical left Protestant theologians than either group is with the conservative wing of its own church. This means that Christianity in Latin America today can be described as having formed three quite distinct camps: the conservative-evangelical Protestants, often called "fundamentalists"; the conservative Catholics of the Establishment; and the radical left-wing group made up of both Protestants and Catholics and characterized generally by secular theology and revolutionary politics. At times the borderlines between them are rather fuzzy, but at least their more typical representatives are quite clearly recognizable.

This book, describing the debate, is not written from a disinterested, unattached, or neutralist point of view. It is intentionally done in more of a journalistic than a scholarly style. It is written so that the majority of Latin American pastors, most of whom have had only six to twelve grades of formal education, can understand the Spanish edition. For English readers, no matter what their academic status, it will serve as an introduction to a field about which very little has yet been written, at least until the much needed scholarly treatment of the subject is produced by someone more qualified. This, incidentally, would best be written by a native Latin American, if possible, not by a "Latin-americanized" gringo.

It is difficult for one who has dedicated his life to the fulfillment of the Great Commission not to take an outspoken position in the debate. When someone writes, for example,

"The idea that the Church's evangelization ought to be reduced to the 'salvation of souls,' understood in the Greek sense, is simply one of the worst heresies that we have to face in our times,"[1] the seriousness of the situation is painted in bold strokes. Regardless of what this author may mean by "the Greek sense," his obvious purpose is to discredit the evangelical emphasis on the doctrine of personal salvation. We are here and now faced with a deep struggle for the faith, with the very life of the church hanging in the balance.

One of the theses of this book is that the theology of the new radical left of Latin American Protestantism is, in its extreme expression, a form of syncretism. The book accepts the challenge thrown out by the Congress on the Church's Worldwide Mission, held at Wheaton in 1966. The 1,000 delegates there declared: "We will acquaint our total leadership more carefully with the religious beliefs and thought-forms of the peoples among whom they live and serve, relative to syncretistic tendencies."[2] As Harold Lindsell says in comment, "If theological syncretism prevails, it will do so because evangelicals have abdicated their responsibilities."[3]

Not only is this book a step toward the direction indicated by Wheaton, but it is also a preliminary attempt to forge a theological point of view on the mission of the church in the world which, if it is not written by a native Latin American, at least is tempered to a large degree by the Latin America in which the author has exercised all thirteen years of his Christian ministry.

Special thanks are expressed to Professor Jack Shepherd, who, in the Fuller Theological Seminary School of World Mission, first inspired this topic. Grateful appreciation also goes to my wife, Doris, who prepared the manuscript for publication.

C. PETER WAGNER
Cochabamba, Bolivia

NOTES TO INTRODUCTION

1. Jorge Pantelís, "La dimensión evangelista de la iglesia," *Avance* (marzo-abril, 1968), p. 2.
2. Harold Lindsell, ed., *The Church's Worldwide Mission* (1966), p. 223.
3. Harold Lindsell, "Attack Syncretism with Dialogue," *Evangelical Missions Quarterly*, III, 4 (Summer, 1967), p. 203.

Chapter 1

THE RISE OF THE NEW RADICAL LEFT IN LATIN AMERICA

It is not always easy to know whether to start with the left or the right. We are choosing the left in the case of Latin American theology, however, because, to begin with, it must be granted that the more liberal elements of Latin American Protestantism have been the first on this continent to emerge with an articulate and reasonably uniform theological position, advocated by a vocal group of church leaders who are Latin Americans by birth.

Many of the more radical of these Latin American theologians have clustered under the umbrella of the Latin American Commission on Church and Society, called "ISAL" after its Spanish initials *(Iglesia y Sociedad en América Latina).* In the official report of its Second Consultation held in 1966, it was claimed that "ISAL achieved the creation . . . not only of a favorable atmosphere for the ecumenical encounter in Latin America, but also a current of theological thought — perhaps the first in the history of Latin American Protestantism — relating specifically to the continent, the major distinctives not being denominational, but rather ecumenical."[1]

For those interested in theological fashions, this achievement merits applause. On the other hand, for those who defend evangelical and Biblical theology as the "faith once delivered to the saints," it is a danger signal. From the beginnings of Protestantism in Latin America around the middle of the last century, the Latin American church has been characterized by conservative evangelical theology. Probably 95 percent or more of Latin American Protestants today could be classified as fundamentalist in doctrine, but ironically their theology has never been billed as "Latin American theology." Instead, the minority composing the radical left has now succeeded to a point in projecting the

11

image of being the depository of legitimate Latin American theology.

How did this happen?

In order to help answer this question, we have, as previously mentioned, decided to start with the left. First we will trace the historical development of this group; then we will examine at close range the theology of its major spokesmen.

Latin America as a Mission Field

While small sparks of Protestantism can be traced back into the sixteenth, seventeenth, and eighteenth centuries in Latin America, these were quickly and effectively extinguished by the all-powerful Church of Rome. Protestantism as a movement did not gain a permanent foothold until the latter part of the nineteenth century. The first of these early Protestants were largely immigrants from northern Europe and England who brought their Lutheran or Anglican chaplains along with them, but who had neither inclination nor desire to engage in missionary work. Many of them had signed agreements with the governments of the countries where they settled not to "proselytize," and the agreements were faithfully kept. Typically the immigrants formed a sealed-off subculture, retaining their Old World way of life and language and maintaining an endogamous community.

Some foreign missions began evangelistic work in Latin America before 1900. These were largely denominational groups, with the Methodist Episcopal Church often taking the lead. The true heroes of the faith in the last century were the colporteurs of the American and British and Foreign Bible Societies, who traveled under indescribable hardships, sold Scriptures, and preached Christ the length and breadth of the continent. The earliest Latin American Protestant churches were founded chiefly in the more liberal republics of Argentina, Uruguay, and Brazil.

When the missionary leaders of the world met in Edinburgh in 1910, Latin America was not even included on the agenda. Since the Roman Catholic Church claimed virtually 100 percent membership there, it was widely considered to be a "Christian" continent. This illusion, however, was much more prevalent in Europe and Britain than in the United States. The proximity of the USA to Latin America permitted North Americans to make a more realistic appraisal of the situation. They were not convinced that outward adherence to Catholic rites made the average Latin American a true Christian. By 1910 a good bit of United States missionary work was already under way in Latin America, and the North Americans were dissatisfied with the Edinburgh attitude. They therefore called their own congress in Panama in 1916. There the debate as to whether Latin America should be considered a Protestant mission field was settled once for all. It was decided to move in with a strong missionary force, and the question was not raised again.

Three major theological and ecclesiastical streams subsequently flowed into Latin America (not including the Seventh-day Adventists, who would probably constitute a fourth). The first was composed of the historical or traditional denominations, which would include Methodists, Presbyterians, Baptists, Lutherans, Disciples of Christ, and others. The second was made up of the newer denominations and societies. The newer denominations, many of which are now affiliated with the Evangelical Foreign Missions Association (EFMA), would be represented by Nazarenes, Church of God Holiness, Christian and Missionary Alliance, Conservative Baptists, etc. The newer societies, largely interdenominational "faith" missions associated together in the Interdenominational Foreign Missions Association (IFMA), included the Central American Mission, Andes Evangelical Mission, Evangelical Union of South America, Latin America Mission, etc. The third stream was composed of several types of Pentecostals. North American Pentecostal groups such as the Assemblies of God, Foursquare Gospel Church, Church of God, etc., have many characteristics of what we have called the newer denominations, and a case could be made for classifying them there. However, the great indigenous Pentecostal churches such as the Methodist Pentecostal Church of Chile are unquestionably in a class by themselves and the picture is somewhat clearer when we group all Pentecostals together as the third stream.

A Persecuted Minority in the Early Decades

In many Latin American countries, professing the Protestant religion was a felony punishable by death in the early days. The liberal wave of enlightenment that swept the continent toward the end of the nineteenth century

13

alleviated the problem somewhat; but nevertheless the first three decades of the twentieth century were a struggle for existence in most places. The Protestant outlook generally was pessimistic. Standing up for the faith meant insults, stones, false accusations, and not infrequently death at the hands of the Catholic persecutors. Only in the more liberal atmosphere of countries such as Uruguay and Argentina could Protestants work in relative freedom.

One of the results of this era of persecution was the development of a polemical theology. Most Protestant theologians and preachers took on the task of exposing the errors of Roman Catholicism with a vengeance. Not only did they denounce such sub-Christian doctrines as the repetition of the sacrifice of Christ in the Mass, the immaculate conception, and the infallibility of the Pope, but they also published scathing exposés of immorality in the convents, abuse of the confessional, and other sins of the flesh that they could attach to the clergy. The polemical approach was followed by all three streams of Protestantism to one degree or another.

Protestantism was not a religion with its own place in the sun during this period. Nominal or fanatic, Latin Americans considered themselves Catholics and their countries as Catholic countries. Protestantism seemed to most people a foreign religion, a heretical and cultic aberration of their own Christian beliefs. It made little sense in their own cultural orientation, and it threatened the status quo. For this reason the approach taken by most missionaries could be described, in Donald McGavran's phrase, as the "one-by-one-against-the-social-tide method." Even today one of the most popular Latin Protestant hymns entones roughly: "My best friends and relatives were turned into enemies when I gave my life to Christ." The Christian road was assumed to be one of inevitable suffering and social ostracism by the majority of Protestants.

These adverse social conditions forced the church to become somewhat withdrawn into itself. For persecuted Christians it was a haven of rest, a center of fellowship with those of like mind, and a balm to troubled souls. Separation from the world and from worldly practices was the order of the day, not only because of social pressures but also because of the strict puritanical orientation of many of the evangelical missionaries. In this struggle for survival there was little time for reflection on the theoretical relationship of the

14

church to the hostile social, economic, or political systems under which it existed. Only on the question of religious liberty did the church make a concerted effort toward political reform, but this was largely a reflex action born of the instinct of self-preservation. Most of the outward energies of the church were dissipated in combatting not the world's social problems, but her ecclesiastical system — Roman Catholicism.

Although it may not be wholly accurate to generalize at this point, it could be said that two discernible approaches to evangelistic work were employed by the Protestant missions at this time. The institutional approach was followed by many of the historic denominations, sometimes with measurable results in church growth, but more often with the major effect being a certain aura of good will being created in the higher level of society to which the hospitals and schools generally ministered. This was justified as a "softening-up process" or as "pre-evangelism." At the same time the newer denominations and the Pentecostals usually created fewer institutions while dedicating more resources to church planting and evangelism.

Some of the graduates of the Protestant schools founded by the historic denominations were offered high-level theological training in seminaries founded for them in Latin America, as well as in seminaries in the USA and Europe. As a result, many of them are today in high positions of leadership. Leadership training in the other groups tended to stress the development of pastors and evangelists, so that these groups are now suffering from a shortage of top-caliber Latin American leadership which can assume positions of influence on the international ecclesiastical level.

The early twentieth century was characterized by a sense of unity among Protestants. This was the type of unity always produced when a common enemy is faced. The tie that binds was at times not so much pro-Protestantism as anti-Catholicism. Today many Christians unrealistically look back on the unity of the early part of this century with great nostalgia, failing to realize that a special set of social and cultural circumstances molded the day. Other quite different circumstances mold today's world. As we shall see, not the least of the newer elements has been the shrinking of the whole world and the subsequent increase in Latin American vulnerability to the winds of influence from outside.

The mood of the Latin American Protestant church changed radically after World War II. A wave of optimism spread across the continent when a large army of new workers and new missionary groups entered to assist those who had been bravely holding the fort. The Roman Catholic Church itself began to evaluate its position in Latin America more realistically and Considine's *Call for Forty Thousand* drew widespread attention to Catholicism's declining vitality. Many Protestant groups enjoyed an upsurge in church growth, and there was reason for encouragement on all sides. Right after the war the Protestant community in Latin America numbered some 1,500,000.

For the first time, the Protestant church could afford the luxury of looking back. As Protestants began to discern the broader outlines of the world in which they lived, they discovered that it was an oversimplification to divide Christians into just Catholics and Protestants. Protestantism itself was a complex mosaic of different emphases. Denominational differences were recognized and often debated. Anti-Catholicism was no longer sufficient grounds for Protestant unity. Positive adherence to other doctrines was beginning to be stressed. International church meetings in Amsterdam and Geneva, Wheaton and Berlin, made their influence felt in Latin America, much to the consternation of many Latins. The idyllic unity of the past began to show some wide cracks.

In the centers of population where the historic denominations had carried on their extensive institutional programs, a new and quite distinct second generation of Protestants began to take positions of leadership. These men, prominent especially in Montevideo, Buenos Aires, and Río de Janeiro, had little interest in the polemical approach of their fathers. They themselves had no first-hand knowledge of Catholicism, and often lacked a radical conversion experience. They therefore became irenic in their attitude toward the Catholic Church. Highly trained in the liberal arts as well as theology, they exerted a good bit of their energies in creative attempts to relate their Protestant faith to their own Latin American cultural milieu. Their ambition, unlike that of the first generation, was to develop an authentic expression of Latin American Protestantism, free from the Anglo-Saxon cultural trappings that the missionaries had attached to it. While

16

this was a good goal, they at times succumbed to the danger of overcompensating in their relationship to the world, and tended to sacrifice the spirit of evangelistic passion of the first generation.

A Respectable Minority in the Wake of Vatican II

When historians evaluate this period a century from now, it may well turn out that Pope John XXIII will have been judged to have had more influence on the Latin American continent than any other man in the twentieth century. Roman Catholicism will never be the same as a result of the council he called and the attitude he infused. Inescapably, Protestantism has also received indelible marks from the turn of events.

For one thing, the polemical approach to preaching and theology is now a thing of the past. Roman Catholics freely admit their mistakes, refer to Protestants as "brethren" (although sometimes still modified by the adjective "separated"), read and preach the Bible, say Mass in Spanish, remove the idols from their temples, and sing Protestant choruses in their "Sunday Schools." In this type of situation there is little room for scolding and scandal-mongering. The Gospel preached must be a positive one. Polemically-oriented literature now gathers dust on the bookstore shelves.

One of the most important effects of this new atmosphere is that it has caused a profound rethinking of the theology of evangelism. While relationships between Protestants and Catholics have perhaps become more comfortable, they have also become more confusing. Perhaps this is the first focal point of the distinction we are attempting to make between the new radical left and the mainstream of Latin American Protestantism. The second-generation Protestants, who had long since left polemics, began calling the Roman Catholics "brethren" in return. But how do you evangelize a "brother"? This is no longer evangelism but "proselytism," and within the new left an aversion to "proselytism" developed as a result of their aversion to polemics. At the same time the majority of Latin American Protestants would not admit that Roman Catholicism was a legitimate expression of Christianity. While not discounting the possibility that some Catholics might be saved, they felt that it was improbable that they would constitute more than a tiny minority in a church that was undeniably better than it used to be, but still decidedly sub-Christian.

Since Vatican II, Protestantism has become socially respectable in most parts of Latin America. Now, more than ever before, one can be a Protestant and still be a good Latin American. It is no longer necessarily considered as either apostasy or a gringo religion.

With this foot in the door of status, some Protestants, especially those of what we are calling the radical left, looked for the opportunity to open it wider. They felt that if Protestantism could gain more status, more Latin Americans might become Protestants. They were convinced that the Protestant church should speak with a louder voice. The increased volume, as we have seen, should no longer be employed in "proselytism," but it could be turned up and beamed toward the issue which at the time was the hottest one on the continent: the social revolution. To develop a theology of social revolution and to involve the church in it seemed to be the most important contribution that Protestantism could make to Latin American society, in the thinking of this group. At just this point the "new radical left" became more clearly defined, and deeply committed to revolution at the same time.

A Vociferous Minority Committed to Revolution

No one familiar with the Latin American scene can doubt that the process of rapid social change has become the most urgent problem of the second half of the twentieth century there. Social revolution is no longer a theoretical option; it is a fact of life. The tremendous changes that began taking place in the economic, political, and social spheres could not be ignored by any responsible segment of society, including Protestantism. The Protestant church is no longer considered a cloister of refuge from a persecuting world; it is, for better or worse, a community that must relate to the world which has accepted it and offered it hospitality. On this all agree.

But when it comes to *how* the church should relate to the current Latin American social scene, differences of opinion enter the picture. One of the most precise classifications of the three major opinions has recently been set forth by William Wipfler, editor of the National Council of Churches' *Latin American News Letter:*

The first is that of the "establishment." It is interested in development and recognizes stability of structures as precondition of development. Whatever measures necessary are justified to provide the necessary stability. The second position, adopted by evolutionists of the liberal tradition, is eager for change, but insists that it be done by whittling away at the barriers and helping to build better facilities to achieve some social justice. The third position is more militant. It consists of those who think that true development requires a break with the present system and the adoption of new forms of social and political organization. Such a radical break is rightly called revolutionary, with proponents more or less prepared to resort to strategies which involve violence. Non-violent revolutionary strategies, of the sort developed in the U. S. racial struggle, have not, to date, captured the imagination of more than a few Latin American leaders. Christians, both Catholic and Protestant, are to be found in each camp.[2]

While it is true these three positions are held by those outside the church as well as those within, our particular interest is their reflection within Protestantism. The new radical left has generally committed itself to the third alternative and the violent, revolutionary expression of it. The theology used to justify this point of view is precisely what will occupy a large part of this book.

Involvement in this particular segment of Latin American Protestantism usually requires several special qualities which all Protestants obviously do not possess. Most likely the exponent of this point of view will be a second-generation Protestant; or if first generation, he probably will not have had a radical conversion experience but will have been "educated" into the church through Protestant schools. He will be a member of one of the historical denominations; or if not, his commitment to the radical position probably can be traced to some special incentive such as a scholarship obtained through one of the historical denominations or some travel funds obtained from ecumenical sources. He will have been trained in one of the more liberal Latin American seminaries such as the Facultad de Teología en Buenos Aires, the Evangelical Seminary of Río Piedras, Puerto Rico, the Presbyterian Seminary of Campinas, Brazil (in one of its periods of liberal domination), the Theological Community of Santiago, Chile, or the like. He will probably have taken graduate work in Europe or the USA in another liberally-oriented seminary on a grant from the World Council of Churches/National Council of Churches (USA). He will play down the persuasive aspects of evangelism, the eschatological elements of final personal judgment, and the heaven-hell alternative as eternal destinies.

The continent-wide structures which have been created as a base for the radical Protestant left are well-financed, skillfully led, and extremely vocal. Most important are ISAL (*Iglesia y Sociedad en América Latina* or Church and Society in Latin America) and MEC (*Movimiento Estudiantil Cristiano* or Student Christian Movement). Of lesser importance for this particular study are ULAJE (*Unidad Latinoamericana de Juventudes Evangélicas* or Latin American Union of Evangelical Youth) and CELADEC (*Comisión Evangélica Latinoamericana de Educación Cristiana* or Latin American Christian Education Council). The master organization to coordinate them all is UNELAM (*Comisión Provisional pro-Unidad Evangélica Latinoamericana* or Provisional Commission for the Promotion of Latin American Evangelical Unity).

Reflected in all of these structures is the deep-seated conviction that the Protestant church should be concerned with treating the open wounds in Latin American society. While these leaders consistently tip their hats to the foreign missionaries who brought the Gospel to their lands, they now feel that only Latin Americans themselves can fully understand the dimensions of their own social problems and move to take the necessary action. In this they are unquestionably right. They admit that plunging into the social revolution as Protestants involves a risk. Whether they realize that this involvement may easily lead to serving mammon rather than serving God is another question. If a syncretism of the Christian message is a necessary measure for this type of involvement, an even greater risk is taken. It is the terrible risk of disobedience to God.

NOTES TO CHAPTER 1

1. ISAL, *América Hoy, acción de Dios y responsabilidad del hombre* (1966), p. 19.
2. William L. Wipfler, "A Column Dedicated to Dialogue," *Latin American News Letter* (December, 1967), p. 9.

Chapter 2

THE THEOLOGY OF THE RADICAL LEFT

No one who reads the writings of the new radical left, much less one who is personally acquainted with its representatives, can doubt the depth of motivation, sincerity of purpose, dedication to high goals, or skill of intellectual analysis of those who have cast their lot on that side. Their interpretation of the relation of the church to the Latin American social revolution springs first and foremost from religious conviction. They are firmly convinced that they are about their Father's business. They are engaged in an intensive search for what they consider to be God's will for themselves, their church, and their countries.

If their understanding of the Biblical world view seems deficient, it is usually not because they fail to acknowledge the authority of the Bible as the Word of God. Although they might not agree with Warfield's view of inspiration, the problem does not lie so much in that area. It lies rather in the extreme degree to which their understanding of the secular world has influenced their understanding of Biblical truth. In many instances (but not all), truth is not denied as much as it is distorted. Priorities are often shifted out of Biblical focus. At times one gets the feeling that the starting point of this group has been an a priori socio-economic theory, and that theology has been called in only as an afterthought, not to say rationalization. The Bible seems to be used very often as a source book for proof texts rather than the touchstone of all doctrine.

The above is admittedly a rather harsh criticism, and it should be pointed out that it does not apply equally to all those who have associated themselves with the radical left. The theological viewpoints spread themselves out in a certain spectrum, and there is some need to classify them in a study like this. Since ideas are inevitably associated with people, it would be impossible to describe them without mentioning names. No

21

personal criticism is intended here. Integrity, sincerity, and devotion are above reproach in these men. Names will be connected with the leading ideas that this research has revealed, but since the research was not completely exhaustive it is altogether possible that I may have missed the mark in certain cases. With some exceptions, the major ideas expressed begin with the more moderate and develop toward the more radical ends of the spectrum.

Before beginning with the specific ideas, it might be well to ask if the theology of the radical left can actually be isolated. It seems that it can. Latin American theology is following the trend toward polarization, which Donald McGavran analyzes in his article, "Missions: Passive and Active." The "passive pole" he describes as:

> Christians who believe that followers of the major religions are going to remain in those religions. . . . In the midst of those blocks of humanity the Christian missionary "witnesses to the reconciling love of Christ," or "is just *there* as Christian presence," or "preaches the Gospel as a witness before our Lord's return," or "serves men quietly in Christ's name," or "enters into dialogue with men of other faiths," or "carries on Christ's ministry of reconciliation."[1]

On the other hand, the Christian who joins others around the "active pole"

> . . . proclaims Jesus Christ as divine and only Saviour and persuades men to become His disciples and responsible members of His Church. The missionary "wins men to Christ," "disciples the nations," "multiplies churches," "propagates the Gospel," "brings nations to faith in Christ". . . .[2]

One of the most concise statements of the mission of the church as conceived of by the new radical left has recently been published in the *International Review of Missions*. The authors are Ricardo A. Chartier of the Facultad Evangélica de Teología of Buenos Aires, Leopoldo Niilus of the Center of Christian Studies in Montevideo, and Carlos M. Sabanes of the Parish-Urban Center of Buenos Aires, all three among the top echelon of the group. Their "concept of mission" includes five points:

(i) The *presence* of Christians and the church in the midst of the daily life and events of secular society.

22

(ii) *Dialogue* or *communication* as a kind of two-way street that makes possible the knowledge of what is really happening to man in society.

(iii) *Participation* or *identification* with those to whom the Gospel is proclaimed or communicated, as an unavoidable consequence of assuming the content and implications of the Incarnation.

(iv) *Service* (diakonia), not as something occasional or optional, but as an essential dimension of the ministry of the church.

(v) The *proclamation* or preaching of the Good News of salvation in all of its rich meaning for the whole life of man.[3]

None of the five points mentioned is a bad idea for the church. All are fine, legitimate Christian activities. But the order in which they appear leaves the impression that they are arranged according to certain priorities. The subsequent development of the *IRM* articles bears this out also, since not once is a burden for making disciples, winning souls to Christ, saving the lost, baptizing new members into the church, or, in a word, fulfilling the Great Commission mentioned. Point v might lead one to think that all this is involved in the mission of the church, but the authors apparently did not have soul-winning evangelism in the forefront.

Instead, their emphasis sounds very much like what McGavran calls the "passive pole." Expressions such as "relate to the Latin American context," "stimulate interest in the study of Christian social responsibility," "undergird involvement in mission by means of studies related to the social, political, economic, and cultural dimensions of the context," "express the growing sense of ecumenical commitment which is inseparably related to the task of mission," "awaken the masses," "point out the roots of the evils in the Latin American socio-economic-political situation," "struggle to remove the principal causes of massive injustice," all are good statements, but the mission of the church — which is to persuade men and women to be reconciled individually to God and to become responsible members of the church of Christ — is not further mentioned.

This is part of what we mean by the theology of the radical left in Latin America. Not only can this line of ideologies be identified, but the persons who hold it have quite generally committed themselves to a circle of ecumenical organizations, theological institutions, and religious publications that are intricately interlocked and therefore also identifiable. This is not a matter of ascribing either guilt or belief by association, but rather a sincere attempt to record the views of Latin American leaders who belong to this emerging fraternity characterized by their inclination toward a secular theological point of view.

Gonzálo Castillo Cárdenas: "Evangelical Transcendence"

Gonzálo Castillo Cárdenas, one of the foremost intellectuals in Latin American Protestantism, was invited to address the World Conference on Church and Society in Geneva in 1966. His paper contains one of the most succinct analyses of the present thinking of the radical left that I have come across. The following statement of the line of reasoning of the left-wing mentality will help establish a base for further study:

> The most important thing in Christianity is love for one's neighbor, because "he who loves his neighbor fulfills the law." This love to be genuine must search for efficacy. If benevolence, alms, a few free schools, a few housing projects, what has been called "charity," be it individual, national or international, does not solve the problems of underdevelopment, we have to look for the efficacious means to do so. The privileged minorities that have the political power are not going to apply these means because generally effective means force minorities to give up their privileges. It is then necessary to take power away from the privileged minorities and give it to the poor majorities. This revolution can be peaceful if the minorities do not resist violently. Revolution is therefore the form of attaining a social orientation that allows the practice of love for one's neighbor, not only in an occasional and transitory way, nor only for a few, but permanently and for the majority of our neighbors. Therefore, revolution is not only permitted, but it is obligatory for those Christians who see it as the only effective way of fulfilling love to one's neighbor.[4]

Castillo's analysis is not designed to provoke theological discussion. It is one reasonable way for a Christian to look at the world around him. We should state at the beginning that we have no theological quarrel with a Christian who feels that political revolution, for example, is one legitimate means to a social, economic, or political end. Pope Paul VI condemned the use of violent revolution in his historic visit to Bogotá, Colombia, in August, 1968, but did not help the unity of his

Catholic Church in Latin America by so doing. North Americans who are heirs to a political tradition that began with a Declaration of Independence stating that when a government becomes destructive of "Life, Liberty and the Pursuit of Happiness, it is their Right, it is their Duty to throw off such Government, and to provide the new Guards for their future Security," have little ground to criticize Latin Americans who today feel the same way.

But the problem runs deeper than political theory. In a magnificent analysis, Castillo outlines three of the major tensions that divide Latin American politico-religious thought. They are: (1) the survival of religious institutions versus the freedom to abandon them and participate in other social institutions instead; (2) Iberian individualism versus social solidarity and national integration; and (3) those who believe in gradual, evolutionary change versus those who advocate revolution.[5] The first point has clear theological overtones. Is the church expendable? Is it just another social institution? Castillo correctly sees this as "basically a theological conflict."[6] On one side, as Castillo points out, there are those who believe that God's interest is focused on the church and that any social order is tolerable as long as the church has freedom to fulfill her mission within it. On the other side, there are those who feel that God's primary concern is for the well-being of mankind, and that any social order which does not promote man's well-being is tyranny, tyranny that must be actively opposed.[7] Castillo goes on to say that there is a

> ...deeper tension between two theologies. One, centered in God, the other centered in man; one integrist and separatist in relation to society in general, the other committed to society as a whole; one attached to dogmatic principles and structures of traditional Christianity, the other committed only to the man, in particular situations. In the words of Teilhard de Chardin: 'Around us the real struggle doesn't take place between believers and non-believers, but between two kinds of believers, two ideals, two concepts of God. A religion of the earth is being formed against the Religion of Heaven.'[8]

What we see here, then, is a conflict between what could be called evangelical Christianity and Christian humanism. It would do us well, however, to keep in mind that the two sides might be talking about something entirely different. When evangelicals begin to formulate their theology, they have evan-

25

gelism in mind as the primary responsibility of the church in the world. Their problem is often that they do not get around to articulating the secondary responsibility of social service with a comparable degree of enthusiasm and skill. But the more radical theologians tend to look at social service as the *primary* responsibility of the church. Unhappily, rather than just bypassing a theology of evangelism they at times set forth an anti-evangelistic theology, as we shall see. From that point of view, they judge evangelical theology not in terms of how true it is to the Bible or how it will result in the salvation of souls, but what it will do to promote social justice.

Castillo, back in 1963, suggested that as far as the church's relationship to the world is concerned, she ought to retain "the dimension of transcendence."[9] The church should neither isolate herself from the world, attempting to restore some romantic image of the past (as the Catholic Church is often prone to do), or make revolution its end. Concerning the last danger, he said that the church should avoid

> ... the temptation to identify the Gospel and the Church, implicitly or explicitly with a given revolutionary program which she sees as indispensable for the establishment of the Kingdom of God on the earth.... I am under the impression that some of the brethren in Cuba fell into that error and now have repented of it.[10]

Castillo's conclusion is one to which evangelicals could confidently subscribe. He says, "The Church has no right to deny her own nature, her divine message, by identifying herself with any human program of social transformation."[11] While individual Christians have a firm responsibility to act in society according to the dictates of their consciences and their political common sense, the church as an institution has neither Biblical mandate nor technical competence to do the same.

It should be noted, however, that Castillo's Geneva address three years later leaned strongly toward secular theology and involvement in the type of violent revolution that the Colombian priest-martyr, Camilo Torres, had advocated. Although Castillo writes in a somewhat vague style, loaded with rhetorical questions, his personal point of view comes through strongly. He asks, "Is it possible to renew the Church without renewing Latin American society? Should not Christians, before all else, struggle for a new social order before attempting to renew the Church?

26

It seems that precisely this is what the Cuban experience can teach the rest of the churches on the continent, for in my opinion, the Cuban Church is passing through a promising renewal which would not have been possible before the revolution."[12]

It appears that Castillo may here have lost sight of the vision he himself projected of "the dimension of transcendence." This is characteristic of the new radical left, which Castillo calls "a growing minority which has opened itself to these problems."[13] These "left-wing Christians," as Castillo calls them, come from "all classic denominations, including Pentecostals and Fundamentalists."[14] The mention of fundamentalists raises some questions, however. If "evangelical transcendence" is practiced, one can understand how a person with evangelical theology might espouse a radical political view. But if radical politics is an inescapable outcome of the Christian theology of mission, as one of the dominant themes of the radical left implies, one might question whether the "fundamentalist" who arrives at that conclusion is a fundamentalist after all.

In other words, we here are beginning to sharpen the true theological question of the day in Latin America. The conflict is not over the person of Christ, the authority of the Word of God, the Virgin Birth, the intercession of the saints, or justification by faith. It is the relationship of the church to the world. As we move on, it will become more and more evident that a Christian can be either a fundamentalist/evangelical or a member of the radical left, but a mixture of both theological points of view is highly improbable.

José Míguez Bonino: "The Intermediate Period"

José Míguez Bonino, until very recently Rector of the Facultad Evangélica de Teología of Buenos Aires, is considered by many as the dean of Latin American theologians. He was the only Latin American chosen as a Protestant observer at Vatican II. Last year he served as guest lecturer at the Union Theological Seminary of New York. He often assumes a mediating position in the Latin American theological dialogue. When he recently addressed a conference of Catholic bishops he suggested that the fundamental-liberal conflict is a "sterile and misguided debate."[15] He agreed with the fundamentalists in their rejection of the naturalization of Christianity and their resistance to the elimination from theology of transcendence, miracle, and divine sovereignty. But he also agreed with the liberals in their opposition to "the narrowing of the Christian faith to the purely individual realm and to the after-death." He applauded their call for "an active participation in society, for the abandonment of the pietistic ghetto, for the proclamation and realization of the social dimension of Christian redemption."[16]

In his desire to rise above what he considers a banal argument, he tends to dismiss perhaps too lightly the theological differences that are a part of the Latin American scene. He says, ". . . We are debating between two heresies: the fundamentalist which tends to ignore the fact that Christ reconciled the world to himself, and the opposite current . . . which fails to recognize the call to faith, conversion, decision, and Biblical eschatology; it seems to ignore the existence of sin . . . it speaks of identification and incarnation irresponsibly . . . ."[17] Míguez would like to dissociate himself from the right and left and stay with the center. If our thesis that Latin American theology is becoming polarized can be borne out, however, he might find himself in a relatively depopulated middle of the road. When Míguez says, "I hate theological labels,"[18] he may be reflecting a certain idyllic wishful thinking.

One of Míguez's characteristic themes is that of the "intermediate time," which he expressed in an ISAL symposium published in 1961 under the title "Biblical and Theological Foundations for the Social Responsibility of the Church."[19]

In his essay, Míguez first outlines the traditional evangelical concept of the Christian in the world, pointing out its strongly eschatological nature. He admits that the Bible teaches that the Kingdom of God comes not through human effort, but by direct intervention of God, that Jesus did not seem too concerned with this present world, and that He taught that His Kingdom was not of this world. The New Testament teaches that the world will get worse and worse until Christ comes as a thief in the night. The Christian is not to be of this world, but a citizen of the heavenly Kingdom. Míguez's understanding of the Biblical and evangelical position is accurate, but strongly critical. He scores this "pietistic" position as "extremely unrealistic."[20] Using this as a point of departure, he develops three major points:

(1) This present age is a time of God's patience; it is an intermediate time. This is why God does not destroy the wicked world. Christ has conquered the world, although His lordship is not yet manifest. God is patient so that the world might hear the Gospel. Order, justice, and peace in the world will allow

the Gospel to be heard better. What, then, should the church do? First-century Christians, being such an insignificant minority, were not responsible for their governments, but today Christians are.[21]

Up to this point most evangelicals agree with Míguez. But his next statement carries some more questionable implications:

> The Church as a Church should become involved . . . so that conditions will be produced in which the Gospel may be freely preached and heard. This concept of "freely preached and heard" is wider than we usually understand it. It does not only take in the minimum conditions for personal security and free speech. It includes the conditions of a "decent human life . . . ," the psychological barriers which create misery and oppression, the injustice, the lawlessness, the insecurity, which for the reception of the Gospel are as real as the suppression of freedom of speech.[22]

Míguez here seems to say that a well-fed and economically secure person is in a better position to hear the Gospel than someone who is poor and oppressed. While we do not mean to say that we should be indifferent to human needs, we would say that affluence does not always and necessarily produce receptivity to the Gospel. Sometimes it is just the opposite. In Bolivia, for example, the oppressed peasants have been more receptive to the Gospel than the wealthy landowners. In India thousands of ragged untouchables have become Christians while very few upper-caste Brahmins have. It is undeniably important that men everywhere have a "decent human life," but this is not necessarily a help to hearing and accepting the Gospel.

(2) The New Testament, according to Míguez, places the responsibility for carrying out God's plan in the world on the church. Therefore, the church must serve the world, not fearing contact with sinners. The church in the world must demonstrate love. True love will not treat man as a "naked soul" but will participate with him in all his problems. This may imply that the Christian will become involved in ambiguous situations, but it is a risk he must take.[23]

(3) What should we expect in this intermediate period? We should not expect that the church will bring in the Kingdom of God, but at the same time we should not limit what Christ can do through the church.[24] The task of participating in the work of redemption involves not only preaching the Gospel, but "participating in the work of Jesus Christ who works in

the world creating peace and order, justice and liberty, dignity and community."[25] This reference to the work of Christ in the world is perhaps one of Míguez's most serious departures from Biblical teaching. One searches the Scriptures in vain to find a commandment that would have Christians move into the world with this kind of mission. To postulate that Christ is hard at work in the world to produce social justice and world peace is to complicate the problem of evil. To suppose that Christ wants His followers, like a mighty army, to join Him in this struggle is to take rather lightly the supernatural forces of darkness that dominate the world in this present age.

This might lead one to suppose that Míguez bypasses the Biblical teaching about the devil, but he does not. In fact, he is the one theologian of those mentioned in this chapter who makes several clear references to the devil. Míguez recognizes the existence of the "forces of evil" in this intermediate period, and uses a figure of Cullmann's to describe him as "the enemy, already defeated, who keeps up his resistance — the hopeless suicidal resistance of a fleeing army." Although the final result is already determined, the "degree of disorder, injustice, oppression, and inhumanity caused by evil is all too evident in the conditions we are well aware of."[26] "We must never forget that Satan does not take vacations," Míguez warns, "and the ambiguity that determines his presence manifests itself also in our situation."[27] Unfortunately Míguez does not outline a clear strategy for combatting this evil power other than cooperation with what he considers to be Christ's action in the world today. The weapons of the radical left seem consistently to be study and analysis, social action and economic reform, revolution and renewal. Seldom are prayer, the Word of God, the preaching of the Gospel, and the work of the Holy Spirit in individual hearts and lives mentioned as valid or useful resources for the Christian in the world. But this does not lessen the truth that "we wrestle not against flesh and blood . . . but against spiritual wickedness in high places"(Eph. 6:12). If the devil is real, and if we take him seriously, no human economic, social, or political scheme will be found adequate to combat him. "Not by might, nor by power, but by my Spirit, saith the Lord of hosts" (Zech. 4:6).

ISAL: "Fear and Trembling"

Although the Latin American Commission on Church and

Society (ISAL) does not pretend to have any official theology, the conclusions of its First Evangelical Consultation on Church and Society held in Huampaní, Peru, in 1961, reflect the general consensus of its members. The statement discusses in detail the Biblical and theological bases for the Christian's participation in politics. The line of reasoning that is dominant in the organization can be summarized in five points:[28]

(1) The primary and fundamental conviction consists of the proposition that "God is present in history, in each concrete situation." God uses historical situations (which apparently are responsive to human initiative) to complete His plan of salvation.

(2) When the Christian comes to recognize this, he is forced to act in the world because God is already acting there.

(3) Discerning God's movements in history requires constant vigilance. To be alert each day to God's action is to live in a tension of "fear and trembling."

(4) At the present time in Latin America, God's work can be identified with the renovation of certain traditional social, economic, and political structures. When, on the other hand, social structures insist on perpetuating themselves, this is to be considered as the work of the devil. In other words, the status quo is one of the world's most evil qualities.

(5) A word of caution. This section of the church, working along with God in the world, will not bring in the Kingdom of God. It may turn demonic if it ever becomes an end in itself.

The statement of "God's presence in the world" is one of the most frequent themes in the theological line we are considering. There would be no problem with this if it were merely a restatement of the Christian doctrine of the sovereignty of God. God is Creator and Lord of the world. He is omnipresent. But something more is meant here. God is said to be acting wherever in the world action is being taken to change society in the direction of a greater measure of what is considered to be liberty and justice. The devil is represented as that force which seeks to perpetuate the oppressive status quo. The church's task in this situation is first to discern the difference through sociological studies, and then to join "God's side."

No wonder this produces "fear and trembling." Even under the generous assumption that the church as an institution would possess the technical competence to judge the world's socio-economic situation accurately, not even the most convinced optimist would suppose that the church could bring its mem-

31

bers to agree to one single political point of view as a possible remedy. Members of the ISAL circle do generally agree with one another, however: Camilo Torres is right, the Alliance for Progress is wrong; God is with Régis Debray, the devil is with René Barrientos; violent revolution is creative, peaceful evolution is unrealistic. But the main line of Latin American Protestantism has not joined forces with ISAL. This is not because they are so much in disagreement with revolutionary theories per se. But they do disagree with the type of spiritual haughtiness that identifies a particular political theory (in this case a Marxoid revolution) with the will of God, and with the type of social action that at times goes so far as to substitute saving society for saving souls. Both are good goals, but if priorities are switched they can easily become wrong.

This is not simply a theoretical possibility when such a line of thinking is carried to its logical conclusion. In some writings of ISAL the social revolution is identified as "also the revolution of the Church."[29] To the degree that the church participates in the social revolution she is doing the will of God. "The impulse which seeks to transform the structures of society . . . is the total, only and true mission, and not only a partial aspect of it."[30] But as Per Lønning asks, "Can a Christian who chooses a particular historical option claim that this is the option Christ makes?"[31] Nothing could stand as a clearer warning of the possibility that the passion for social action can become such a strong drive that it inverts Biblical priorities. "Fear and trembling" should characterize Christians not in relationship to the risk of jumping into ambiguous worldly situations, but in relationship to the possibility of failing to make the offer of salvation available to mankind. As Paul said, "Woe to me if I preach not the Gospel."

While God is omnipotent and omniscient, He has allowed Satan to become in some sense "the god of this age" and "the prince of the power of the air." If God has determined that today's world be a garden of justice and peace, but if it has not been so ever since the fall of Adam, His very omnipotence is called into question. If it is answered that God intends an earthly utopia, but only to the extent that it can be realized through the church, two observations can be made. First, we look in vain for this teaching in the New Testament. Nowhere is the church commanded to change society in such a specific way; but she is commanded to make disciples, reconcile men and women to Jesus Christ, and baptize those who accept the Son of God

32

into the church. Secondly, even if changing society is assumed as a legitimate ministry of the church, logic would indicate that the best way to go about it would be to make the church grow so that it becomes more than a poor and insignificant minority. The church is the salt of the earth, but trying to salt down an entire beef carcass with a table-sized salt shaker would be futile and unrealistic. Not even the Communist guerrillas are this naive. They realize that unless their program of subversion begins to recruit the peasants of their victim country, their guerrilla band will come to naught as it did in Bolivia under Ché Guevara in 1967. Unjust people cannot produce a just society. Regeneration is needed to conquer unrighteousness.

Ricardo Chartier: "Extension of the Incarnation"

The professor of Christian Social Ethics in Buenos Aires' Facultad Evangélica de Teología, Ricardo Chartier, although a North American, is one of the most frequent contributors to the radical left literature in Spanish. He sets forth his views concerning the relationship of the church to the world in a series of twelve propositions, leading, as do almost all roads of the radical left, to revolution. Chartier's twelve steps can be summarized as follows:[32]

(1) The church must exhibit a high quality of internal life as the koinonia of the gathered community of believers. They are the "people of God."

(2) Since the church is "the extension of the incarnation," however, this koinonia must have an orientation "not primarily interior, but exterior," toward the community rather than toward the church herself.

(3) The church that truly believes in the Incarnation will begin its ministry by establishing valid contact with the world around it, and living in it.

(4) The church must know the world well. It needs to make an exact evaluation of the world in general and its own community in particular.

(5) "The incarnation . . . signifies identification and solidarity . . . as 'our world,' not the world 'of others.' It is necessary that the church become an 'instrument for God's redemption in the world.' "

(6) Once established, the church should act as "the conscience of the society" or exercise "prophetic criticism" of the society.

(7) The local church should have a social ministry, which carries its own justification as diakonia and is not necessarily planned to create a better receptivity of the Gospel.

(8) The church should serve society wherever it goes as "the scattered Church."

(9) The church should exercise responsible citizenship.

(10) Belief in the Incarnation should impel the church to work toward uniting a fragmented society.

(11) The church should promote community social service.

(12) But the "most decisive and most demanding" responsibility of the church in the world is to "transform the structures of society in order to obtain a responsible society, characterized by liberty, justice and order."

While many questions are raised by Chartier's exposition, most of them are commented on in other sections. The special emphasis here is his concept of the church as the "extension of the incarnation." This theme often recurs in the writings of the radical left. Chartier gives no Biblical or theological reasons for holding this position, taking for granted perhaps that his readers will agree. But it is a doubtful premise. The term "incarnation" has traditionally signified God's taking on human flesh in the person of Jesus Christ, and there is no Biblical warrant to assume that the church possesses this quality of her Lord. Nor is there any linguistic warrant to alter what Christians have always meant by "incarnation." While the church is described in the Bible as the "body of Christ," Paul obviously has no intention that this should be understood metaphysically but rather metaphorically. The same would apply to the church as Christ's bride or as "the household of God." The church, rather than being *vere deus*, as Christ was in the Incarnation, is an embarrassingly weak and unworthy servant who can at best make a faltering attempt to obey the commands of her Lord and Master, the truly Incarnate One. He has commanded this servant, as the parable of the great feast indicates, to go out to every social class with the invitation to the wedding banquet. He desires that the church move out into the world to win receptive multitudes and that His "house be filled."

In this sense, Chartier makes a helpful comment when he says that our church structures are often introverted. They are "structures for 'coming' (the people come to church) and not for 'going' (the church goes out to meet the people)."[33] This criticism of church structures would be admitted by most Christians. The disagreement enters when we ask what the church says to the people once she finds them in the world. One searches Chartier's writings in vain to find a reference to the preaching of the cross, the call to personal repentance, the making of disciples, and their baptism in the name of the Trinity. He disappointingly suggests social action as "the extension of Christian ethics and faith into society."[34]

This is perhaps why, in his chapter in the ISAL book *Responsabilidad social del cristiano*, he discusses koinonia and diakonia, but never gets around to even mentioning kerygma. In a sense he feels that a strong showing in social service (diakonia) in itself is preaching the Gospel, and therefore no special emphasis on the proclamation itself (kerygma) is called for. "This diakonia," Chartier says, "is an expression of Christian faith that declares the nature of God and His redemptive activity in living terms."[35] Diakonia is a good and necessary function of the church in the world, but only a sub-Biblical theology of mission would develop the concept without assigning it a position in the total mission secondary to that of kerygma.

Joaquín Beato: "The Prophetic Mission of the Church"

Closely related to Chartier is Joaquín Beato's plea that the church today exercise a ministry parallel to that of the Old Testament prophets. He feels that this prophetic mission involves chiefly the "offer of an interpretation of the historical revolutionary movement in which we live, in the light of God's total purpose."[36] One would wish that Beato would define more clearly what he believes the total purpose of God in the world to be. His article does not mention reconciling lost sinners to God. He does not relate God's purpose in the world to sin, repentance, or the new birth. According to Beato, the church must "claim the totality of life and human relations for the Sovereignty of God." Christians should concern themselves with acting "as a mouthpiece and mediator for the humble, for those who have been placed in an inferior status by an evil social order, thus testifying of the special interest God has for them."[37]

The above phrases describe lofty and noble principles. Every Christian should share the burden of the humble and poor. But they tend to cloud rather than clarify the issue. Beato's phrase, "the world, whether it wants to be or not, whether it knows it or not, is under the dominion of Christ,"[38] raises many questions. No one doubts that God is the sovereign Creator of the world. But to assert His present action in the world in Beato's terms may be an oversimplification. The temptation to hide from the ugly facts of sin, evil, and a personal devil, powerful and rampant in today's world, is all too great. They complicate the issue. Rarely among the representatives of the radical left does one come upon a real concern for the wickedness of the unregenerate heart and the recognition that it can be changed only through the regenerative power of the Holy Spirit.

While the Scriptures teach us that God is sovereign, they also teach that this sovereignty will not be manifested in its fullness throughout the world until His second coming (parousia). To postulate that the mission of the church is somehow to bring the world under the sovereignty of God through social action and previous to the parousia is well-intentioned, but as ill-directed as Peter's attempt to protect our Lord by cutting off the ear of His adversary.

Beato voices his opposition to the present social structures of Latin America, and most Christians would agree that they leave much to be desired. Many would also agree that these should be done away with and replaced by new structures. How this should be accomplished is a matter of debate among evangelical Christians in Latin America. But Beato attempts to derive a *political* conclusion from *theological* premises by indicating that social structures should be judged by Christians as good or bad on the basis of how they "fulfill the redemptive purpose of God."[39] Is it possible that social structures *ever* do this? What is the "redemptive purpose of God in this world"? This is one of the key issues in the analysis of Latin American theology. It leads us to the next section, which is one of the most crucial.

Valdo Galland: "Cosmic Redemption"

"Cosmic redemption" is a major theological building block for many of the theologians of the radical left. Perhaps for our purposes Uruguayan Valdo Galland will serve as one of its most typical exponents.

It should be noted first that the word "reconciliation" often comes up in the writings of the radical left in a political rather than a spiritual context. This is closely related to the concept of redemption. When four top Latin American leaders drew up a statement protesting the U.S. invasion of the Dominican Republic in 1965, reconciliation was a key term. "The specific contribution which Christians should make at this decisive moment is the costly exercise of the ministry of reconciliation," they said. "Who can speak of reconciliation at this hour, if not he who reconciled the world to himself by the sacrifice of the cross?" According to them, "the concrete significance that the ministry of reconciliation assumes in the present hour is to recognize our own guilt and the guilt of our governments."[40] Here reconciliation is not thought of as persuading a sinful man to be reconciled to his God. It is rather the reconciliation of two opposing social and/or political forces with each other.

Galland, who headed up the Latin American Student Christian Federation (MEC) before moving to Geneva and then to New York where he is WCC Secretary for Mission and Service, gives us a tightly reasoned argument for "cosmic redemption" on Biblical and theological bases.[41] His premises and logic are quite typical of the thinking of the radical left. The argument is summarized as follows:

> (1) Christ's death on the cross is a "complete victory because through his full identification with men, his death has vicarious value for all" (Col. 2:15; 2 Cor. 5:19).
>
> (2) The cross defeated the powers of evil, but final victory will come in the parousia.
>
> (3) Meanwhile, 2 Peter 3:9 teaches that we live in the time of God's patience, of God's building His church and of the church's mission to make disciples.
>
> (4) But other than this, God also works outside of the church. He uses natural and sociological powers to accomplish His work in the world.
>
> (5) Here we see the cosmic dimensions of Christ's work. "He did not come just to save individuals, but to redeem the whole world" (Col. 1:19-20). "This cosmic redemption is also taking place now. . . . It follows that human works and institutions are capable of redemption; they can be brought within the Christian dispensation and directed not merely by natural ethics, but by the ethics of the Gospel. . . . What have been called 'the intellectual gospel' and 'the social gospel' are constituent elements of the task of the church."
>
> (6) The Protestant church has "not been able to avoid irresponsible individualism in which there is great concern for the believer's own blessedness and carelessness for the life of the world."

Up to point three, Galland has set forth a pattern that most Latin American Protestants fully accept. But when he makes the attempt to extend the benefits of redemption to the world in a realized as contrasted to a potential sense, he moves to questionable theological ground. While Galland does admit that the church should be built and extended, others who follow the "cosmic redemption" line to a more radical extreme doubt that the church is relevant in our day. Tomas Liggett, who for many years headed the Río Piedras Seminary in Puerto Rico, looks upon the nineteenth-century church as under the influence of "individualism, puritanism and pietism," and as such "tending to see her mission in terms of fulfilling the Great Commission."[42] He implies that this is antiquated, and sees a more up-to-date picture for the twentieth century. Society, not the individual, is now of supreme importance. Therefore the focal point of the church's action in the world should no longer be individuals, but social units. "The redemptive action of God," he says, "is to produce a cosmic redemption in which all things will be reunited in Christ.... The church should *testify* of this redemption and the lordship of Christ in man, society, history, the world, and the universe."[43] Liggett does retain "proclamation" as a part of the mission of the church, and he even holds that evangelism is the main dimension of mission, although he would add testimony, communion, and service to the total mission of the church.

The emphasis that evangelism is the main task of the church is important. Some other representatives of the radical left have lost it. If the church keeps in the forefront her commission to persuade men and women to commit themselves to Christ, she does well. Nevertheless, there is doubt that the Bible uses the word "redemption" in the context of bringing social structures under the umbrella of Christian ethics, although undoubtedly the world would be better off for it. This will be the case during the millennium, but not before. One of the most serious dangers facing the Christian church today is to divert valuable resources that could otherwise be used in winning multitudes to Jesus Christ to idealistic social projects which will win few if any, and which are predestined even to social failure before they begin. As Aharon Sapsezian observes, new social and economic structures "carry buried within themselves the seed of their own corruption."[44] This does not excuse the church from diakonia, but simply attempts to set the diakonia in proper theological perspective. Kerygma, not diakonia, is God's instrument to make His redemption efficacious to man in the world.

Cosmic redemption often leads to one more theological danger that should be mentioned. If Christ redeemed the whole world, the question arises as to whether anyone really is lost. While it is true that the majority of the world's population has never been confronted with the claims of Christ, how do these people relate to a cosmic redemption? Not all representatives of the Latin American radical left would say that they are really in Christ whether they know it or not, as would D. T. Niles, for example. Many of them would refuse to discuss the problem on the grounds of its being irrelevant to the great issues of the day. Unfortunately, a book published by ISAL expresses ideas perilously close to a type of universalism that would consider all men saved and thereby eliminate any need for the type of evangelism that persuades men to become Christians. Two of the prominent passages follow:

> Bonhoeffer begins his study on the activity (of Christians in an "adult" world) on the basis that God has redeemed in Christ all those who have separated themselves from Him in sin.[45]

> The redemptive purpose of God in Jesus Christ is universal, as universal as the creation, as universal as the person of Christ.[46]

It cannot be denied that God *desires* that all men come to repentance. But this must not cause us to lose sight of the equally Biblical fact that all men do not come to repentance and that they are "condemned already." The eschatological implications of this need to be stressed much more in Latin American theology. We will return to the problem of quasi-universalism in a later section.

Justo González: "The Sacrament of Social Service"

In his book *Revolución y Encarnación (Revolution and Incarnation)*, Justo L. González of the Río Piedras Seminary of Puerto Rico expresses his aversion to that type of Christianity which is so detached from the world that it is introverted and consequently does little good for others. He is disgusted with "those who think that Christianity satisfies no more than the needs of the soul."[47] Much of his indignation is well justified, for although there is a widespread movement throughout the Protestant church in Latin America to become more involved in social action, hundreds of churches remain socially indifferent.

As is often the case, however, the healthy initial reaction to a deficiency that has been observed in church life, leads in turn to an unhealthy overreaction.

First of all, Gonzalez' judgment of those who do not agree with him may be a little harsh. He attempts to charge them with the heresy of Docetism, which became prevalent when gnostic philosophy invaded the church in the second century. Docetists held to a metaphysical dualism in which all matter was considered evil per se. If Christ's body were matter, they reasoned, Christ could not have been sinless; therefore since He *was* sinless, His body could not have been real matter. In a word, they could not accept the doctrine that Christ was really man.

Whereas González charges no one with a metaphysical dualism, he does state that "we fall into a practical Docetism which is a negation of the incarnation of Christ."[48] Here González begins to reflect a view of the extension of the Incarnation similar to Chartier's. "This Docetism," he continues, "is characterized by a spiritualistic interpretation of Christianity."[49] He suggests that to avoid Docetism we take seriously the relationship of God with the world since the Incarnation and "thus arrive at a *Christian materialism*."[50]

One theological danger involved in this formation of a "Christian materialism" is an exaggeration of the immanence of God. At times it leads to a neglecting of the supernatural and transcendent aspects of God's relationship to the world and to humanity. González thinks that "Christianity does not pretend to find God outside of material realities, but rather sees Him within those very realities."[51] He mentions that the Bible is "paper and ink," but fails to come to grips with balancing that self-evident characteristic with its supernatural qualities. He does avoid the obvious and potentially devastating conclusion of pantheism, however, by stating clearly: "God *is not* these realities, but *He gives Himself to us* in them."[52]

Following his attempt to prove that his opponents are Docetists, González proceeds to the effort to raise his own particular theological insight to the level of sacrament. He considers the social work of the church as important as its sacraments. Since the Reformers said that the church could be identified wherever the Word was preached and the sacraments administered, González apparently feels that he can convince the church that social service is an urgent necessity by proving it to be a sacrament.

In order to do this, he decides to start with a "redefinition of the concept of sacrament" so that it is more clearly related

40

to the "fundamental doctrine of the incarnation."[53] This will help lead us to an understanding of "how God acts in history and thus the way that we as His children should act in it."[54]

Negatively, González says that a sacrament "is not an act of magic," nor is it "a simple psychological exercise." Positively, a sacrament is "one of those historic moments which God has chosen in order to make Himself known to us."[55] Among the many possibilities that this definition could open up to the theologically imaginative, González discovers his "sacrament of service."

If González has been successful in showing that social service is a sacrament of the church, his further conclusions follow logically. "We cannot separate ourselves from Christian service without ceasing to be Christians," he says. The presence of sacraments is one of the identifying signs of the church, so he can say that "without the Scriptures, without the Church, without the sacraments, it is impossible to be a Christian, since these are the means that our Lord has established through which he comes to us. Likewise, he who neglects Christian service — as he who neglects the Lord's table — neglects the Lord himself."[56] González comes to the conclusion that service to fellow men is the raison d'etre of the Christian church.

Few would disagree that the church must reach out in service or else become stagnated, ingrown, and a failure in her mission to the world. But service to mankind usually carries the implication of the only unique contribution that the church is qualified to make to the world, that of preaching the Gospel and persuading lost sinners to be reconciled to God through Christ. This, however, is precisely what González does *not* want to be interpreted to mean. He clarifies the issue by saying, "When we speak of the 'sacrament of service' we do not refer simply to the service of preaching the Word, but we also refer — and this above all else — to the Christian service that seeks to satisfy the physical and social needs of our neighbor."[57]

Rubem Alvez: "The Church as a Grain of Wheat"

The strong emphasis of the radical left on social and physical, in contrast to individual and spiritual needs, leads some, like Brazil's Rubem Alvez, to scold Christians for preaching a gospel of individual salvation. He pleads for a "reformulation of our programs of evangelization."[58] He is particularly disturbed by the type of evangelism he calls "proselytism," which he feels leads to a spirit of competition between groups. Although he does not mention it, as a Latin American he undoubtedly would be referring to preaching to Roman Catholics with the objective of bringing them into the Protestant church. He does not agree that the church should interpret evangelism as persuading man that they should repent of their sins and be born again, but rather to "announce the reality of the power of God, present and operating, transforming the confusion of history according to his loving purposes."[59] He, like Justo González, says that "the social ministry of the local church has a *sacramental character*."[60]

Alvez does not seem much disturbed by the haunting contradiction in a philosophy of history that indicates that for at least twenty centuries God has been hard at work trying to "humanize mankind," but apparently with little success. Two world wars, Korea, Hungary, Viet Nam, Biafra, Czechoslovakia — all are dirty smudges on the twentieth-century world's canvas. If God is the artist, a more complete and satisfactory explanation must be given of the blotches of mud, hair, and filth that soil what vestiges of the good, true, and beautiful can still at times be discerned. Alvez's exposition of the "forces that oppose the action of God" does not come to grips with the Biblical concept of a temporal spiritual dualism in which the supernatural forces of evil play a sinister and important part. He rather searches for natural causes of evil:

> The forces of disintegration are established on all levels of life, bringing about the dehumanization of man, the corruption of all kingdoms whether it mean the kingdom of man's relationship to man or that of man's relationship to nature.[61]

Why doesn't Alvez mention man's relationship to God? The Bible places this first and foremost: "Seek ye first the kingdom of God and His righteousness." He is not impressed by the idea. His solution to the problems mentioned above is that the church get on with the revolution. "The action of God signifies revolution in the most radical sense of the word, and therefore the Christian community can never identify itself with the *status quo*."[62] He echoes Justo González' charge of heresy against the more moderate wing of the church. He scores the "stereotyped answer" of the conservatives that the Gospel is truly revolutionary, but "naturally a spiritual revolution." "In this type of answer we find the roots of the modern docetism of the Protestant Church."[63]

The "penultimate character" of the revolution scares many Christians away from it, says Alvez. He distinguishes between the "ultimate" and the "penultimate" in this manner:

> I said that Marxism is a symbol, that is, the penultimate. Let us keep in mind that the horizontal dimensions of life permit only penultimate or provisional reality. Whatever is provisional causes a human predicament. Nothing in this world has to do with the ultimate or the absolute. If something is ultimate or absolute in the Christian faith it is a miracle, an exception, an invasion.[64]

The ultimate became the penultimate in the Incarnation, according to Alvez. "God became man, identifying himself with all the precariousness of the human situation in order to redeem it."[65] The conclusion is that "the church is obligated to run the risk of associating herself with all those who are involved in the humanizing revolution. Only from this position can she hope to be heard."[66] A more specific identification of this "movement toward humanization" is "that which has Marxism as its catalytic agent," Alvez asserts.[67]

Notice how Alvez reverses the Biblical "ultimate" and "penultimate." The Bible naturally recognizes that man is not, as someone has facetiously said, "a soul with ears." It recognizes man's need of food, drink, clothing and shelter. It recognizes that every man has a right to share the physical and material blessings of nature, and that social justice is a worthy goal. But the order again is important. The Bible does not indicate that Christians should fight in the Marxist revolution, or should agitate in labor unions, or should publish self-righteous declarations against the large world powers, and then "all these things shall be added unto you." If the Incarnation means anything, it at least means that Christians should obey the words of the Master who said, "Seek ye *first* the kingdom of God." Any other point of view risks disobedience to God.

We have already mentioned that Alvez recognizes the risk for the church that involvement in the Marxist-catalyzed revolution carries with it. But he takes this risk to an extreme that only a certain group of the radical left shares. He believes that it might be a good thing if the church went completely out of existence. This is the anti-ecclesiastical "grain of wheat" theory, which suggests that if the church die and is buried, God will raise up something better in the future, as He did with Christ. It would be well to capture Alvez's extended thinking on the point:

> In order to impart life to the world, the church should remember that she is challenged to renounce her own life for the world's benefit. A grain of wheat remains alone unless it falls into the ground and dies. But if it dies it produces a rich harvest. The church cannot avoid such a risk when it is playing with matters of life and death. Whenever the purpose of God for man and society is found in danger, the church should assume the risk and be crucified. This crucifixion can appear to be a total defeat. According to human standards, the church may have come to its end. She has to face the reality of the captivity. But only by this pathway, the pathway of risk, can she find security. Only through captivity can she become free, only through death can she begin to live; to live truly not for her own self, but for the world.[68]

The emphasis that this point of view gives to the absolute necessity of the church's expending every bit of her energy in service in the world is good. No believer should count the cost of saving the world, for as Paul said, "necessity is laid upon me." However, the evident burden of the New Testament is not for the *death* of the church, but rather for the *growth* of the church. Christ went on to the cross in order to purchase His bride, His "pearl of great price," and He never hints that He also would want His bride to go to the cross. His commandment to His church was to preach the Gospel of the Kingdom so that the Kingdom could multiply throughout the world like the mustard tree or like the leaven that penetrates the whole mass. Neither the mustard seed nor the leaven is described as dying, but rather as multiplying.

One of the most telling criticisms of the point of view that the church exists not for itself, but to serve secular society, has been written by Norwegian Per Lønning. He points out that the idea underlying the statement "that Christ is the servant and the incognito" lacks meaning unless it is "combined with the proclamation of Christ as the Risen Lord." He goes on to say:

> If Christ came only to serve in humility and anonymity, his logical goal could only have been oblivion. And if his main activity today is to set man free through the process of "de-

sacralization" and secularization, and if he refuses to claim authority over the thoughts of men, the most efficient contribution the church could make to his mission would be to stop talking about him.[69]

There is much in the idea of the "extension of the incarnation," as Ricardo Chartier expresses the nature of the church, which may be instructive for Christians. Philippians 2 is clear in the sense that Christ's attitude of humility and self-sacrifice should be ours also, although, as we have seen, Chartier's ideas raise some questions. On the other hand, even making the church the "extension of the incarnation" falls far short of making the church the "extension of the crucifixion." It is hoped that this extreme, by no means common in Latin America, will prove, like the "death of God" in the USA, to be a passing theological novelty.

Jorge Lara Braud: "Solidarity with the World"

Jorge Lara Braud, a Mexican intellectual currently directing the Hispanic-American Institute in Austin, Texas, hits the mark when he states, "The theological issue . . . is precisely the Church's relation to the world."[70] Lara would agree basically with others of the radical left that the church, as an extension of the Incarnation, is the agent for God's cosmic redemption in the world. He asserts, "The sovereignty of Jesus Christ in the world signifies that the situation *extra-ecclesiam* has never been without the tempering presence of the Lord of lords. . . ."[71]

Over and above what has been stated concerning previous authors, however, Lara finds an implication in the doctrine of the relation of the church to the world that the others have not stressed. His insight concerns the "solidarity of the Church with the world." Lara reasons as follows:

> The incarnation of God in the world establishes the world "as the theater of God's glory" (Calvin). As far back as the calling of Abraham, the inseparability between the Church and the world was ordained. . . . If God is sovereign over both the Church and the world, then their solidarity is established . . . . Hence, the Church has life in the measure in which it lives for those outside it. Conversely, the Church ceases to have life in the measure in which it tries to save it.[72]

Solidarity between the church and the world is easier to demonstrate from the Old Testament than it is from the New, although even there, outside of Israel herself, there is little indication of either desire or fulfillment of solidarity with the world at large. Our Lord said that He was "not of the world," and that those whom the Father gave Him were "not of the world" (John 17:16). "The world hath hated them" because God's children are not part of it (John 17:14). Believers were given to Christ from "out of the world" (John 17:6). John commands Christians to "love not the world, neither the things that are in the world. If any man love the world, the love of the Father is not in him" (1 John 2:15). Such texts hardly lend themselves to a concept of "solidarity."

It is true, however, that Jesus also said, "As thou hast sent me into the world, even so have I also sent them into the world" (John 17:18). We should note two things about Jesus' involvement in the world that the church should imitate. In the first place, Jesus never partook of the sin of the world. He associated with drunkards, but he never got drunk. He associated with adulterers, but never committed adultery. He associated with thieves, but never stole. If the church is to be effective in the world today, she must move freely in the world, but avoid its contamination just as Jesus did. Some may object that this is "pietism." So be it. It is a wholesome and necessary aspect of pietism.

The second thing about Jesus' involvement in the world was His purpose. "For the Son of man is come to seek and to save that which was lost" (Luke 19:10). He was the shepherd who desired to gather straying sheep into His fold. He wept over Jerusalem, not because of its poverty or social injustice or racial prejudice, but because its inhabitants resisted His Gospel and would not come to Him as the responsive Galileans did. Jesus sent His disciples out into the world for the primary purpose of making more disciples and baptizing them into the Church (Matt. 28:19-20).

This last point is important because Lara, for example, in his enthusiasm to establish a solidarity with the world, is in danger of losing sight of the purpose Christ has in sending His disciples into the world. In a paper written in 1967 he expresses an aversion to the stress that some place on the conversion experience because:

For one thing, it sanctifies a simplistic scheme of "life in the Gospel" against life in the world, which fails to see the social

> dimension of God's Good News for the world, and which creates
> a pharasitical separation from the very ones whom the Gospel
> calls us to serve . . . . it is simply not true that conversion . . .
> puts an end to . . . man's solidarity with the world.[73]

While the church unquestionably needs to maintain a social witness in the world, if overenthusiasm for it obscures or dilutes the message of reconciliation of individual men and women to God through Jesus Christ, the danger flag is raised.

Dana Green, head of the National Council of Churches' Latin American Department, says that since the churches do not take their solidarity with the world seriously enough, "socially concerned Christians from Pentecostalists to Roman Catholics are finding a church outside the churches."[74] This is an intriguing concept. He labels it the "church in Diaspora." This church is to "be presented to the world as nothing more and nothing less than one of the many instruments which God may use in accomplishing His purposes in the world."[75] Green sounds as if he means that the church is just another social institution. The question, of course, is raised as to who are the members of this "church outside the churches"? Do they serve God or mammon? If God's purpose in the world is to redeem lost sinners, only those who are already redeemed can do the job. Otherwise we inevitably will find the blind attempting to lead the blind, and both of them falling into the ditch.

It should be mentioned before passing on, that Lara has a good bit of reason for suggesting a closer relationship of evangelicals to the world in a good sense of the concept. He and William Wonderly of the American Bible Society made an extensive survey of evangelicals in Mexico City, publishing their results in 1964.[76] This survey showed that evangelicals had tended to make the separation from the world so abrupt that they lost contact with a world that could otherwise have provided them with bridges to carry them into evangelistic opportunities. They pointed out that some Protestants had "cut the lines of effective communication with neighbors and relatives to whom, if they could have shared common problems and interests, they could have presented Christ and His Gospel with much more relevance."[77] It is true that if a Christian loses contact with the world, the effectiveness of his ministry is reduced proportionately. This will be developed further in Chapter 6. But one wonders if the phrase "solidarity with the world" is really the most helpful one that could be devised to correct the error.

Emilio Castro: "Constructing the Earthly City"

The organizers of the 1966 World Council of Churches Conference on Church and Society held in Geneva, chose Uruguayan Methodist Emilio Castro to bring the opening devotional message. In doing so they selected the man undoubtedly considered the foremost leader of the ecumenical movement in Latin America. His position of Coordinator of the WCC-encouraged UNELAM committee is well-earned and places him in the forefront of the left-wing element of Protestantism. Harold Lindsell of *Christianity Today* mentioned the name of only one Latin American in his report of the 1968 WCC Assembly in Uppsala, the name of Emilio Castro. Lindsell said:

> The assembly was equally forthright in its appeal to conservative evangelicals to find their places in the WCC structures. At the moment the WCC has its eyes on the Pentecostals, particularly in Latin America. At a meeting scheduled for 1969 it will once again try to get the ecumenical ship afloat there, under the leadership of Emilio Castro. Previous attempts have failed.[78]

Castro is so prolific that a whole book could be written about him alone. This brief investigation turned up eighteen books, chapters, and articles that he has written in both English and Spanish. Castro travels widely and mixes with all kinds of people. As pastor of the First Methodist Church in Montevideo, he keeps in close contact with the man in the pew. As Executive Secretary of ASIT (the theological education association of the southern part of the continent), he rubs shoulders with the top theological educators. He is a competent observer of the social and political scene as well as a recognized theologian, having studied under Karl Barth.

The Geneva Conference has gained a certain degree of renown as being quite a radical gathering. In his message to the delegates there, Castro undoubtedly found himself in step with the spirit of the day. His sermon, entitled "The Perspective of the Cross," followed much the line of thinking brought out in the earlier section on Rubem Alvez concerning what we have called "the church as the extension of the crucifixion." The cross leads

Castro to postulate that it might not be such a bad idea for the church herself to end her existence, at least the church as we know it today. He says:

> If our Lord went to the cross, surrendering his own life with complete self-sacrifice for the blessing of mankind, what other course can the church take, save to follow in the steps of its own Lord? We are not here to ask ourselves how the church can preserve its own ways, or how it can survive in a new age; we are here to ask how the church can forget itself and contribute in some way to the salvation of men all over the world. The cross reminds us that when we speak of economic, sociological or political problems, we are speaking of the men and women who Jesus Christ regarded as his own brothers once and for all when he accepted the cross.[79]

Of course, if Castro is not concerned with church survival, he is much less concerned with church growth. Rather than commenting on his views on church growth here, however, we will save them for the next chapter.

If the church is considered as the heavenly city, or at least its provisional manifestation in the world today, one wonders what Castro would substitute for it if he were successful in tearing it down. In a paper presented to a top-level meeting of ecclesiastical leaders from the USA and Latin America in Bogotá in the same year, he expounded the theory of an "earthly city":

> Theological reflection brings us and lifts us to the comprehension of the building of the earthly city as the fundamental Christian task. Instead of seeing the world as the spring-board from which the soul jumps to the beatified situation, it discerns the interest of God in the whole scenario to assure for man the conditions of liberty and responsibility which express his character as a son of God and his capacity for an authentic decision before the same God. The task of constructing the earthly city is not a task of the conversion of souls. There is no conversion of souls that is not in the forefront of the fight for the construction of the earthly city.[80]

Most evangelicals, reading a paragraph like this, think it is nonsense. Conversion is commonly believed to be the entrance into the heavenly, not the earthly, city. But the key to Castro's thinking is an understanding of what he means by "conversion."

He developed this in a paper entitled "Conversion and Social

Transformation," at a Congress on Evangelization held in Co-chabamba, Bolivia, also in 1966. While he confesses his belief in personal salvation, he expresses his deep concern about the fact that most people who have a conversion experience do not participate in the social revolution that surrounds them. "The person who experiences conversion to Christ passes through an initial period of revolutionary inhibition," he says. "Social change frightens him."[81]

Conversion, for Castro, should involve participation in social movements. "There is no such thing as conversion for personal benefit," he says.[82] By this he means that not only is a person's relationship to Christ changed through conversion, but that the person should begin doing in the world just what Christ is doing in the world. What is Christ doing in the world then? Most Latin American evangelicals would answer that He is sending forth His disciples to fulfill the Great Commission. Castro would not disagree with that, but he states that "the Great Commission, the announcement of the Gospel, should be understood also in community terms."[83] Castro seldom stresses the centrality of individual repentance of sins, the necessity of personal regeneration by the Holy Spirit, or the will of God that multitudes should be baptized into the church.

In some of his writings, he seems to have an aversion to a soul-saving ministry. He criticizes his opponents' hypothesis that "if we change the heart of man, the society will also change," by asserting that "No such thing as the heart of man exists."[84] This leads him at times to set up an improbable dichotomy between being saved and making an honest and worthwhile contribution to the society in which one lives. He asks whether the Christian in a revolutionary setting "should isolate himself, take refuge in personal piety, flee the inevitable contamination, in search of his own salvation"?[85] This is set forth as one alternative, which he then contrasts to social action. In other words take your choice: either be a separated Christian or be involved in helping your fellow man.

But there is no need to set personal salvation over against participation in social and political affairs. Many fine Christians live a pious life, "work out their own salvation in fear and trembling," but still make their Christian contribution to society. Faithful Christians do not flee the world and isolate themselves as Castro suggests. They carry out their Christian witness in the world without fear or embarrassment.

One of the problems with many of those who want to tear

down the heavenly city and build an earthly one is that they are committed to one particular method of construction — that of violent revolution. As we have said before, a case should not be made to *exclude* this possibility from the list of options available to a Christian who sincerely wishes to arrive at the best solutions to the social and economic problems of his particular country. If a Christian wants to join the revolutionary party, that should be his prerogative. But if we arrive at the conclusion that the only true Christian is the one who has immersed himself in the revolution by saying, "We truly announce Jesus Christ only if we are in the midst of the social revolution,"[86] we come dangerously close to depriving Christianity of its transcendence and making it just another social institution.

The European point of view that sees the church as a state church and precisely as a social institution should not have much influence in Latin America where the typical church is not a lazy and ingrown social institution but rather a living and growing organism in the midst of a society that traditionally has been hostile. The theology of those who have been conditioned by the ecclesiastical situation of the liberal River Plate area is vulnerable at this point. Some of the second-generation Protestant churches are very European. It becomes even more evident in those theologians who have taken advanced degrees either in Europe or in the older seminaries of the USA. Emilio Castro reflects this to a certain extent when he says in a sermon:

> Where are the whores and the publicans today? Where are the social parasites of our day? Are they within or without the Church of Jesus Christ? Do they feel welcome to the Church of Jesus Christ or rejected by the implicit decency of the Church? To ask the question is to answer it: the Church has suffered a process of "decentizing" as the centuries have gone by.[87]

Sociologists such as Emilio Willems and Christian Lalive have reported, on the other hand, that precisely the level of society to which the rapidly growing churches of Brazil and Chile, for example, are appealing is that lower level. Undoubtedly the members of the Jotabeche Pentecostal Church of Santiago, Chile, would not feel at home in Montevideo's First Methodist. Those who have been converted in Santiago count the whores, the publicans, and the social parasites among themselves.

Castro is strongly critical of this kind of church, which he

51

calls the "come here" church. He is disturbed by the preaching of the Gospel in doctrinal terms: man is a sinner, the wages of sin is death in hell, Christ paid for his sin with His shed blood, repentance and faith are needed to be saved, etc. "The Church, when it reduces its message to doctrinal formulations . . . has annulled its own proclamation,"[88] Castro says. In another place he develops the idea more fully:

> The Christian mission in such circumstances cannot be an act of transmitting a series of doctrinal affirmations, not even the attempt to translate those affirmations for the man of today. Rather it must be an effort to place itself in the situation of that man in such a manner as to gain the opportunity to be heard and perhaps understood, through service and sacrifice.[89]

The message of these churches is naturally closely related to the *methods* used to spread the message in the world. In describing them, Castro emerges with a caricature of what he terms "the more evangelistic churches":

> Their program is fulfilled with the preparation of their members to move out and look for new members. They have a great evangelistic task, but also with the benefits of future members in mind. They are concerned with the growth of the church and the salvation of souls. The world is the hunting ground where God's hunters (or fishermen) search for their prey. Joy is complete when they stay in the Church and the process begins again with new hunters. They admit that many hunters are lost along the pathway, and that the community in which they move considers them as proselytizing groups, more interested in institutional growth than in the fulfillment of their responsibilities as citizens.[90]

Castro places himself on the side of presence theology ("The mission of the Church is the presence of Jesus Christ in the world")[91] and of secular theology ("The coming of Jesus Christ into the world is a secular event, not a religious one").[92] He also leads, in some of his writings, into what might be termed an incipient universalism. In this he often sounds like a Latin American, D. T. Niles.

His idea of the work of Christ in the world reconciling all things to Himself, is one of the theological starting points. This has been developed in the section on Valdo Galland, so there is no need to repeat it here. The danger of universalism was pointed out there, and some stronger signs of it are found in Castro. This is not to say that Castro is a true-blue universalist, but certain statements that he makes cause doubts in the minds of conservative evangelicals. In his most extensive treatment of the subject we have come across, he begins by affirming his belief in "evangelism." "Nothing in what we are able to write or think as a result of this research on the mission of the Church, should cut the wings of a powerful evangelization."[93] He then mentions that Christ came for all men. "He came to give His life. God has no children or stepchildren. His gracious action tends to benefit the whole of humanity. In every man He is active through His Holy Spirit."[94]

To bolster his point of showing God's special interest for those outside of His chosen people, he reviews what God did with Melchizedek, Ruth, Cyrus, and the wise men. Then, "in the person of Jesus of Nazareth is where we most clearly see this universal interest of God."[95] God's love, according to Castro, includes all men somehow in Christ. "What happens in Christ has its implications for all men. It is no longer possible to consider any man, or even the history of mankind, as independent of Jesus Christ. Whether the world knows it or not, it is already conditioned by the marvelous fact of this love made flesh in Jesus Christ . . . . In Jesus Christ God accepts all of humanity."[96]

Castro does not attempt at this point to relate his theory of all of humanity being accepted by God through Christ with the Biblical passages that mention the reality of hell, the division of the human race between those who are "in Adam" and those "in Christ," and the desperate urgency for those outside of Christ to hear the Gospel.

He approaches the heart of the issue by asking: "What is the final destiny of those who die without having known the name of Christ?" but he never satisfactorily answers the question he raises. He does hint, however, that we need not be too concerned, for "in the New Testament and in the Old Testament there are clear indications for us to affirm that the plan of God in Jesus Christ incorporates all humanity."[97]

Richard Shaull: "Death and Resurrection of the Logos"

In spite of the fact that he is a North American, Princeton Seminary Professor of Ecumenics Richard Shaull is considered a legitimate and articulate spokesman for the Latin American left. During his years as MEC (Student Christian Movement) leader and theological professor in Presbyterian Seminaries in Brazil, he left a permanent impression. He still spends much time in Latin America. In the final report of the Second Consultation of ISAL (Church and Society) in El Tabo, Chile, the editor mentions that it would be difficult to single out individuals who made contributions with one exception, Shaull:

> One name that without any doubt should be singled out is that of Richard Shaull, who in a ubiquitous and heterogenous participation, contributed to the consultations, study groups, and institutes organized by ISAL.[98]

In many respects he is the most extreme, but at the same time he is the most profound and the most prolific of the group. Although the sources for this analysis are not exhaustive, they nevertheless show a development of thought in Shaull that parallels to a certain degree the thinking of the whole school.

Back in 1953, Shaull's writings were fairly evangelical. In struggling with the relationship of proselytism to evangelism, for example, he still advocated "an encounter with the living Lord," "a personal decision before Him," and "that the student who has been converted . . . become an active member of a permanent and vital Christian fellowship."[99] Then by 1955 he was developing the idea of God's speaking to us "in the events of history," which must be seen through "the eyes of faith."[100] This is the beginning of a process of secularization of theology in which Shaull came to see human institutions as expressions of man's sin and a subsequent need for God to pronounce judgment on them and offer "salvation" to the social structures themselves. The decisive action of the church in the world today, he now believes, is not to convert men to faith in Jesus Christ as personal Lord of their lives, but to "repent." Repentance means to Shaull, "to hear what God is saying to us in the events of history, see our involvement in all that is being judged, and change our ways so that we may become the bearers of God's purpose for the world"[101] "Changing our ways," like "turning over a new leaf," is a concept of the result of repentance that falls somewhat short of the supernatural regeneration of the Bible.

Shaull's thought has advanced, within the last two or three years, to what may be considered quite a high degree of secularization of theology. He believes that religion "in a past age" helped man to "reach a higher grade of humanity." But "in the present we can only reach a full understanding of what is human to the degree that we advance toward the secular; when we reach that liberty which permits us to see above those myths created by man and by which he has lived."[102] He now feels that the mission of the church is not to extend itself, but is "that of being present on those frontiers as a witness to what Christ is doing and to the possibilities he opens for man in that situation."[103] We should not expect all those who accept Christian principles to seek membership in the church. "Our *Christian* concern," he affirms, "is for the shaping of an authentic *secular* existence."[104]

Although Shaull tips his hat to "the pioneers of a former day,"[105] he quickly asserts that today "we do not have the same objectives." One of his most graphic and iconoclastic passages states that:

> We can no longer think exclusively in terms of rescuing lost pagans from the imminent flames of hell. The missionary today may not have too great an opportunity for direct evangelism though his work is no less important for the proclamation of Gospel. And most of us do not feel that we do justice to the Biblical faith if we limit it to providing people with an entrance ticket to heaven.[106]

With this rejection of the eschatological urgency of the mission of the church in the world, Shaull makes a decisive break from evangelical theology. It is quite remarkable that he feels that by rejecting the urgency of saving people from hell he is being faithful to the Bible. One wonders if Bonhoeffer's exaggerated emphasis on the Old Testament has not caused New Testament theology to become so diluted among secular theologians that the terrifying thought of a human being cast into the lake of fire no longer has as much power to move the heart as does a ragged peasant who has become disinherited by moving into a *favela*.

Although he has little to do with Latin America (he lectured once at an ISAL workshop in Buenos Aires), it would be well to indicate that perhaps the best-known secular theologian of them all, Harvey Cox, agrees with Shaull and reinforces what he says. According to Cox:

> The starting point for any theology of the church today must be a theology of social change. The church is first of all a respond-

ing community, a people whose task it is to discern the action of God in the world and join in His work.[107]

In the secular city Cox discerns the "same eschatological reality once expressed by the idea of the Kingdom of God."[108] Cox sees the kerygmatic function of the church as "broadcasting the seizure of power" with the message of the fact that a revolution is under way and that the pivotal battle has already taken place."[109]

In the 1966 Geneva Church and Society Conference (from which we have already quoted Castillo and Castro), Shaull expounded his radical views in a hard-hitting argument. In many respects it is a classic statement of the theological mood of the Latin American left, although many would not yet endorse all his ideas. Shaull quotes Arthur Rich as saying that:

> Christian existence is revolutionary existence, and the Church's service to the world is that of being the "pioneer of every social reform" without making any claims for Christianity or trying to Christianize the revolution.[110]

Then Shaull affirms, "I find myself obligated theologically to support (this interpretation) and rejoice in it."

At this point Shaull sets forth his characteristic "death and resurrection of the Logos" theory. This, he feels, is "the only road open to us in this situation." By it he means that Christian theology, like the Logos, should die and expect to be resurrected in some new and creative form. For example:

> (1) Our traditional discussions about God, His otherness and His sovereignty, make little sense today, but we can describe the freedom, openness and hope that are possible in a world over which He is Lord.
> (2) A new generation may not pay attention to our former complicated discussions of eschatology, but they might be interested in an apocalyptic perspective of . . . the present world that combined a sense of urgency about revolutionary change, and acceptance of the possibility of deepening crisis and tension in the present order, and expectant appropriation of new possibilities precisely in the midst of this crisis.
> (3) We may not talk much about Jesus Christ, but we can point to his concrete benefits in the midst of our lives today.[111]

The idea about being in the world without talking about

Christ has a great appeal to those whose orientation is toward the European type of state church which is just another institution, and a weak one at that. Shaull refers to Bonhoeffer, who of course lived in such a context in Germany, but whose experience could hardly speak to Latin America, except perhaps for some of the atypical Latin American churches of the second and third generations. He says, "Just as Bonhoeffer saw, religion in our days has come to be, for a large group of persons, a sphere outside experience, completely foreign to daily life."[112] This may help explain why Shaull is so anxious to do away with the traditional theological terminology:

> Almost all the terms which have had traditional validity in theological thought — including those that refer to God, to salvation, etc. — are now identified with a bygone world. They no longer hold any meaning for those who are concerned with the present situation.[113]

He suggests that theology be crucified, and that "out of this openness to crucifixion, a new theological resurrection may once again take place."[114] Then he joins Rubem Alvez and Emilio Castro in their desire that "the church should be free at all times to follow, if necessary, the path of crucifixion."[115]

Such pessimism might be justified in the Latin American context if the church were going downhill like she seems to be doing in Europe and the United States, but with a growth rate of 3.33 times that of the population, this is not the case.[116] It is a shame that such a pessimistic view of the church is being accepted by some outside of Latin America as representative of Protestant Christianity there.

As an alternate viewpoint to that of church growth, Shaull suggests with others that the church should be considered "in the Diaspora." Old church structures will no longer suffice, so the church should now "take on forms of solidarity with man in his struggle to obtain and maintain the 'humanity' of human life."[117] So closely should the church identify with the secular world that the "distinction between believer and unbeliever" is really an "obstacle to our evangelistic action."[118] This idea of a "community of believers" is wrong to Shaull because it detracts from a concern for the whole man. In order to prove his point, he states that "Jesus Himself didn't seem to make any special effort to constitute a community of those who, as a result of His ministry, received pardon or believed in Him."[119]

From this Shaull proceeds to do a curious thing. He mis-quotes Scripture so as to make the words of our Lord seem to support what he is contending about the church. He quotes the Great Commission in these words:

> Go ye therefore and make disciples in the name of the Father and of the Son and of the Holy Ghost; teaching them to ob-serve all things whatsoever I have commanded you: and lo, I am with you always, even to the end of the world (Matt. 28: 19-20).[120]

Unless this could be a misprint, the omission of the words "bap-tizing them" constitutes not only a violation of God's Word, but an offense to the canons of responsible scholarship. The sacrament of baptism, of course, indicates entrance into the church as a "community of believers," against Shaull's theory. He does not discuss the passage in which Christ states "upon this rock I will build my church" (Matt. 18:18), obviously an-other reference that the disciples who gathered in Jerusalem after the ascension took to mean a "community of believers."

Once he abandons the concept of the church in its present form, Shaull is left only with the world as the context in which the individual Christian must act. According to Shaull, the Christian should not make the mistake of imposing his pre-conceived ideas as to what the world might need upon a world that already has a negative predisposition toward Christianity. To him, the best approach is to let the world tell him what it wants and what it wants him to do about it. As J. G. Davies of Birmingham University said in a series of lectures given in Bolivia, "The Church ought to let the world give her the plan of action; give her the agenda."[121] Shaull, in turn, suggests that:

> Our task is not to improve certain values, but rather to recog-nize and live according to the world's values; it is not to give meaning to life, but rather to discover the meaning of life in a world that is participating in redemption; it is not to establish order in the universe, but rather to participate in the new or-der of things taking shape through social transformation.[122]

This process of casting oneself upon the world is one of the terrifying extremes of radical theology that the Latin American conservative evangelicals fear. The Protestant church in Latin America was born, not because the missionary pioneers asked the world for an agenda, but because the Bible had already given them a commission. Had they asked the Latin American world to furnish them with a plan of action, fifteen million Latin American Protestants might still be waiting to hear the Gospel.

A Word About Marxism

Shaull's political views are closely related to his secular ecclesiology. His present revolutionary stance raises the question of the element of Marxism in Latin American secular theology. This is a very delicate point, and one upon which a nonspecialist should avoid making pontifical judgments. But it is a matter that cannot be omitted from a book of this nature, even if the treatment of it is admittedly incomplete.

Back in 1963 Shaull was not yet convinced that Marxism was the answer to Latin America's social problems. "Marxism has not yet demonstrated that it is capable of creating a new society which takes into consideration the deepest aspirations of the masses."[123] After a visit behind the iron curtain, Emilio Castro admitted that even in the countries where the revolution has occurred, the Christian church has hard sledding. "There is no liberty to propagate Christian teaching or other manifestations of religion," Castro says; "The visible and obvious goal is to impregnate society with the idea of a world in which religion has no place."[124] Shaull himself does not hesitate to say that "the Russian experience might indicate that the revolution also can become a dehumanizing force."[125]

It is a risk to pin the label of "Marxist" on any of the representatives of the new radical left. But it would be safe to say that a Marxist-oriented ideology has at least as much influence on some of them as the Bible. Whether a person can be a Marxist and a Christian at the same time is one of those thorny and virtually unanswerable questions. Shaull leans toward the position that such a combination is possible in an article on Nicholas Berdaiev, whom he calls a "Christian thinker."[126] Others believe that "Marxist" and "Christian" are self-excluding terms.

After criticizing certain weaknesses of Marxism, Shaull goes on to admit that Marxist ideology "is essential today as an instrument for the social revolution."[127] He would give priority to "awakening the rural and urban masses from their traditional lethargy."[128] Marxism is considered to be the most probable political option in today's world to solve the social problems created by four centuries of colonialism and imperialism in Latin America. Therefore "there is no reason why we should consider it our mission to keep the new Christian and Marxist leaders from taking power and developing new economic and political structures in an attempt to solve their countries' problems."[129]

The prevalence of this opinion throughout the radical left of Latin American Protestantism may be seen in the publication of such titles as *Christian Faith and Marxism*,[130] *Man, Ideology and Revolution in Latin America*,[131] and *The Influence of the United States in Latin America*.[132] It is what prompts José Míguez to praise guerrilla-priest Camilo Torres,[133] Ricardo Chartier to introduce the Latin American church to Saul Alinsky,[134] and Hiber Conteris to write:

> These events prove that the possibility in which many of us had placed our hopes up until a short time ago, that is, that the inevitable transformation of Latin American structures will come about in a rapid, but not violent, manner, without a sudden collapse of traditional society, has practically disappeared. The change will probably be delayed longer, but it will have to come through the revolution and with a huge outburst of violence. This revolution will contain forces which are not necessarily Marxist, but ... which will have lost all contact with traditional society.[135]

Marxist ideology in the left wing of the church is a fact of life in Latin America. At its deepest levels it tends toward a deficient anthropology. Some view man as "the creator of his own history, for good or for bad."[136] Although attempts are made to disguise it, man is frequently conceived of in naturalistic terms, and man's problems described in imminent categories. The precarious relationship of sinful man to a transcendent God is not a frequent theme. Redemption is usually viewed in the horizontal man-to-man or society-to-society dimension rather than in the vertical man-to-God dimension. The problem lies not only in a variation of emphases between the two dimensions, but in the almost total indifference to the vertical.

In an attempt to relate the Marxist view of man to the Christian, Julio Barreiro concludes that the basic conflict lies in the difference between "naturalism and incarnation." He says:

> While the Marxist . . . places all his emphasis on human natural-
> ism, the Christian, without negating that, puts all his emphasis
> on Christ made man.[137]

Since Barreiro only develops the thought on the horizontal level of the Christian's responsibility to carry the consequences of the Incarnation "into the heart of society," one is tempted to suspect that such references to Christ as above are a type of pious smoke screen raised around a sub-Biblical concept of man. New Testament theology describes man's most basic need in terms of sin, repentance, and regeneration. Until these are adequately dealt with, it is hardly possible to develop a valid Christian anthropology.

The two folk heroes of the Latin American Marxist-oriented sector are martyrs Camilo Torres and Ché Guevara. Torres, a priest who turned into a guerrilla fighter, made a statement when he left the priesthood that has served as an inspiring test to all Christian leftists ever since. He said:

> I have left the privileges and duties of the clergy, but I have not left the priesthood. I believe to have devoted myself to the revolution out of love for my neighbor. I will not say the Mass, but I will realize this love to my neighbor in the temporal, eco-nomic and social realms. When my neighbor has nothing against me, when I have realized the revolution, I will then say the Holy Mass again. Thus I believe to obey Christ's command, "If you are offering your gift on the altar and remember that your neighbor has something against you, leave your gift before the altar and go; first be reconciled to your neighbor, and then come offer your gift."[138]

Shaull's recent statement is more concise, but seems to reflect the sentiments of Camilo Torres. He declares: "Having spent most of my life working for reform within the established order, I am now obliged to give priority to revolution."[139]

The important issue is not really whether a Christian can hold a Marxist-oriented political ideology or not. The issue is whether Christianity obliges a man set free in Christ to hold to *any predetermined* ideology at all. The Christian world view transcends all social, economic, and political systems. As long as a Christian's goals in his relationship to the world are noble and held with a clean conscience, he should be allowed to choose the political means to reach the goals that he feels are best without his very Christianity being called into question.

This applies equally to the capitalist and the socialist, the pacifist and the violent revolutionary. Samuel Escobar sums up the matter well when he says:

> The Christian's liberty emerges from the fact that he knows that no economic or political system is "Christian," and that the destiny of the Church of Christ is not tied in with any particular society or manner of life.[140]

NOTES TO CHAPTER 2

1. Donald A. McGavran, "Missions: Passive and Active," *The Presbyterian Journal* (August 2, 1967), p. 9.
2. *Ibid.*
3. Ricardo A. Chartier, *et al.*, "Missionary Structures and Training for Mission — The River Plate Area," *International Review of Missions,* LVII, 226 (April, 1968), p. 218.
4. Gonzálo Castillo Cárdenas, "Christians and the Struggle for a New Social Order in Latin America" (1966), pp. 5-6.
5. *Ibid.*, pp. 4-5.
6. *Ibid.*, p. 5.
7. *Ibid.*
8. *Ibid.*, p. 6.
9. Gonzálo Castillo Cárdenas, "El desafío de la América Latina a las iglesias evangélicas," *La naturaleza de la iglesia y su misión en Latinoamérica*(1963), p. 42.
10. *Ibid.*, pp. 43-44.
11. *Ibid.*, p. 44.
12. Gonzálo Castillo Cárdenas, "Los cristianos y la lucha por un nuevo orden social en América Latina," *Cristianismo y Sociedad,* IV, 12 (1966), p. 88.
13. *Ibid.*, p. 89.
14. *Ibid.*, p. 93.
15. José Míguez Bonino, "Main Currents of Protestantism," *Integration of Man and Society in Latin America,* p. 196.
16. *Ibid.*
17. José Míguez Bonino, "Un Dios que actúa y renueva la iglesia," *América Hoy* (1966), p. 54.
18. José Míguez Bonino, "Nuestro Mensaje," *Cristo la esperanza para América Latina* (1962), p. 72.
19. José Míguez Bonino, "Fundamentos bíblicos y teológicos de la responsabilidad social de la iglesia," *Encuentro y Desafío* (1961), pp. 19-26.
20. José Míguez Bonino, "Fundamentos teológicos de la responsabilidad social de la iglesia," *Responsabilidad social del cristiano* (1964), p. 24.
21. Míguez, "Fundamentos bíblicos y teológicos de la responsabilidad social de la iglesia," p. 22.
22. *Ibid.*, pp. 22-23.
23. *Ibid.*, pp. 23-25.
24. *Ibid.*, p. 26.
25. Míguez, "Fundamentos teológicos de la responsabilidad social de la iglesia," p. 29.
26. *Ibid.*, p. 28.

27. Míguez, "Un Dios que actúa y renueva la iglesia," p. 54.
28. Iglesia y Sociedad en América Latina, *Encuentro y Desafío* (1961), pp. 40-42.
29. Iglesia y Sociedad en América Latina, *América Hoy, acción de Dios y responsabilidad del hombre* (1966), p. 16.
30. *Ibid.*, pp. 16-17.
31. Per Lønning, "The Theological Basis of the Geneva Conference," *Christian Century* (March 1, 1967), p. 271.
32. Ricardo Chartier, "Modos de la relación entre la iglesia y la sociedad," *Cristianismo y Sociedad*, Año I, No. 2 (1963), p. 63.
33. Ricardo Chartier, "La iglesia en una sociedad en transformación," *Id por el mundo* (1966), pp. 5-13.
34. *Ibid.*, p. 82.
35. Ricardo Chartier, "Relaciones entre la iglesia y la sociedad," *Responsabilidad social del cristiano* (1964), p. 51.
36. Joaquín Beato, "La misión profética de la iglesia evangélica en América Latina," *La naturaleza de la iglesia y su misión en Latinoamérica* (1963), p. 27.
37. *Ibid.*, pp. 27-28.
38. Joaquín Beato, "Ideología Cristá como base para a acao social de Igreja," *Cristianismo y Sociedad*, I, 1 (1963), p. 16.
39. Beato, "La misión profética de la iglesia evangélica en América Latina," pp. 27-28.
40. Luis Odell, *et al.*, "How Latin America Sees it," *Christian Century*, LXXXII, 25 (June 23, 1965), p. 806.
41. Valdo Galland, "God's Present Work in Latin America," Chapter 1 of *Raise the Signal* (1961), H. S. Converse, ed., pp. 30-38.
42. Tomas Liggett, "El evangelio y la misión de la iglesia," *La naturaleza de la iglesia y su misión en Latinoamérica* (1963), p. 80.
43. *Ibid.*, p. 81.
44. Aharon Sapsezian, "The Emerging Sense of National Identity," Chapter 6 of *Raise the Signal* (1961), H. S. Converse, ed., p. 103.
45. Iglesia y Sociedad en América Latina, *La responsabilidad social del cristiano: guia de estudios* (1964), p. 36.
46. *Ibid.*, p. 27.
47. Justo L. González, *Revolución y encarnación* (1965), p. 39.
48. *Ibid.*, p. 22.
49. *Ibid.*
50. *Ibid.*, p. 23.
51. *Ibid.*, p. 24.
52. *Ibid.*
53. *Ibid.*, p. 30.
54. *Ibid.*
55. *Ibid.*, pp. 30-31.
56. *Ibid.*, p. 36.
57. *Ibid.*, pp. 41-42.
58. Rubem Alvez, "El ministerio social de la iglesia local," *Responsabilidad social del cristiano* (1964), p. 60.
59. *Ibid.*
60. *Ibid.*
61. Rubem Alvez, "Injusticia y rebelión," *Cristianismo y Sociedad*, Año II, No. 6 (1964), p. 48.

62. *Ibid.*
63. *Ibid.*
64. *Ibid.*, p. 51.
65. *Ibid.*
66. *Ibid.*, p. 52.
67. *Ibid.*, p. 51.
68. *Ibid.*, p. 53.
69. Lønning, *op. cit.*, p. 271.
70. Jorge Lara Braud, "Latin America's Challenge to the Church — the Issues We Face" (1966), p. 2.
71. William L. Wonderly and Jorge Lara Braud, *Los evangélicos somos así* (1964), p. 54.
72. Lara, *op. cit.*, p. 3.
73. Jorge Lara Braud, "Protestants and the Process of Integration," *Integration of Man and Society in Latin America*, p. 210.
74. *Ibid.*, p. 8.
75. *Ibid.*, p. 9.
76. Wonderly and Lara, *op. cit.*
77. *Ibid.*, p. 54.
78. Harold Lindsell, "Uppsala 1968," *Christianity Today* (August 16, 1968), p. 6.
79. Emilio Castro, "The Perspective of the Cross," *Study Encounter*, 3, 3 (1966), pp. 107-108.
80. Emilio Castro, "Protestants in the Latin American Revolution" (Oct., 1966), p. 4.
81. Emilio Castro, "Conversión y transformación social" (1966), p. 10.
82. *Ibid.*, p. 5.
83. Emilio Castro, "Nuestra tarea inconclusa," *Cristo, la esperanza para América Latina* (1962), pp. 97-98.
84. Castro, "Conversión y transformación social," p. 2.
85. Emilio Castro, *Misión, presencia y diálogo* (1964), p. 14.
86. Emilio Castro, "En busca de la estructura misionera de la congregación," *Cuadernos Teológicos*, XIII, 3 (1964), p. 85.
87. Emilio Castro, *Cuando molesta la conciencia . . .* (1962), p. 88.
88. Emilio Castro, "Misión y evangelización," *Id por el mundo* (1966), p. 19.
89. Castro, *Misión, presencia y diálogo*, p. xii.
90. Castro, "En busca de la estructura misionera de la congregación," p. 84.
91. *Ibid.*, p. 85.
92. Castro, "Misión y evangelización," p. 22.
93. *Ibid.*, p. 21.
94. *Ibid.*
95. *Ibid.*, p. 23.
96. *Ibid.*, p. 24.
97. *Ibid.*, p. 25.
98. Iglesia y Sociedad en América Latina, *América Hoy, acción de Dios y responsabilidad del hombre*, p. 19.
99. Richard Shaull, "Evangelism and Proselytism in Latin America," *Student World*, 46, 1 (1953), pp. 18-19.
100. Richard Shaull, *Encounter with Revolution* (1955), pp. 61-62.
101. *Ibid.*, p. 2.
102. Richard Shaull, "Y un Dios que actúa y transforma la historia," *América Hoy* (1966), p. 65.

103. Richard Shaull, "Toward a Reformation of Objectives," chapter in *Protestant Crosscurrents in Mission, The Ecumenical-Conservative Encounter* (1968), p. 98.

104. *Ibid.*

105. Shaull, *Encounter with Revolution*, p. 144.

106. *Ibid.*

107. Harvey Cox, *The Secular City* (1965), p. 108.

108. *Ibid.*, p. 110.

109. *Ibid.*, p. 124.

110. Richard Shaull, "The Revolutionary Challenge to Church and Theology," *Princeton Seminary Bulletin*, 60, 1 (October, 1966), p. 30.

111. *Ibid.*, p. 30.

112. Shaull, "Y un Dios que actúa y transforma la historia," p. 58.

113. *Ibid.*

114. Shaull, "The Revolutionary Challenge to Church and Theology," p. 32.

115. Shaull, "Toward a Reformation of Objectives," p. 95.

116. William R. Read, Victor M. Monterroso, and Harmon A. Johnson, *Latin American Church Growth*, p. 55.

117. Richard Shaull, "La forma de la iglesia en la nueva diáspora," *Cristianismo y Sociedad*, Año II, No. 6 (1964), p. 13.

118. *Ibid.*, p. 15.

119. *Ibid.*, p. 16.

120. *Ibid.*

121. J. G. Davies, *Diálogo con el mundo* (1967), p. 73.

122. Richard Shaull, "Una perspectiva cristiana del desarrollo histórico y social," *Hombre, ideología y revolución en América Latina* (1965), p. 79.

123. Richard Shaull, "Recientes estudios sobre el desarrollo político en Asia, Africa, y América Latina," *Cristianismo y Sociedad*, Año 1, No. 2 (1963), p. 50.

124. Emilio Castro, "Posibilidad de la fe en los países socialistas," *El Predicador Evangélico*, XXII, 88 (1965), p. 248.

125. Richard Shaull, "Ideología, fe y revolución social," *Testimonium*, X, 2 (1964), p. 43.

126. Richard Shaull, "Hacia una perspectiva cristiana de la revolución social — Nicolás Berdaiev," *Cristianismo y Sociedad*, III, 7 (1965), p. 6.

127. Shaull, "Ideología, fe y revolución social," p. 43.

128. Richard Shaull, "The New Latin Revolutionaries and the U.S.," *Christian Century*, LXXXV, 3 (January 17, 1968), p. 69.

129. *Ibid.*, p. 70.

130. Hiber Conteris, ed., *Fe cristiana y marxismo* (1965).

131. Hiber Conteris, ed., *Hombre, Ideología, y Revolución en América Latina* (1965).

132. Pablo Franco, "La influencia de los Estados Unidos en América Latina," *Cristianismo y Sociedad*, V, 13 (1967).

133. José Míguez Bonino, "Christians and the Political Revolution," *Risk*, Stephen C. Ross, ed., 1-2 (1967), pp. 100-110.

134. Ricardo Chartier, "Saul Alinsky: el conflicto y la controversia en la organización de la comunidad," *Cristianismo y Sociedad*, Año V, No. 14 (1967).

135. Hiber Conteris, "El rol de la Iglesia en el cambio social de América Latina," *Cristianismo y Sociedad*, III, 7 (1965), p. 57.

136. Julio Barreiro, "La naturaleza del hombre en Marx," *Hombre, Ideología y Revolución en América Latina* (1965), p. 38.

137. *Ibid.*, p. 39.

138. Castillo, "Christians and the Struggle for a New Social Order in Latin America," pp. 3-4.

139. Richard Shaull, "Revolution: Heritage and Contemporary Option," Part Two of *Containment and Change* (1967), by Carl Oglesby and Richard Shaull, p. 183.

140. Samuel Escobar, "Diálogo entre Cristo y Marx," *Certeza*, 7, 25 (enero-marzo, 1966), p. 8.

Chapter 3

RADICAL THEOLOGY
AND CHURCH GROWTH

The July, 1968, issue of *International Review of Missions* was dedicated in its entirety to "Church Growth." Ten, or even five, years ago, only an elite among mission leaders understood the special significance that this term has now acquired. Today it is a household word among Protestants engaged in missions, evangelism, and church work. Its apostle is Dr. Donald McGavran, Dean of the School of World Mission and Institute of Church Growth at Fuller Theological Seminary. McGavran's book *Bridges of God,* published first in 1955, was the *magna carta* of the church growth movement. In his introduction to the book, Kenneth Grubb shrewdly observed that it was "a tract for the times." Since then, McGavran has written such books as *How Churches Grow,* and edited *Church Growth and Christian Mission,* as well as having produced innumerable articles in the widest variety of religious periodicals. The *Church Growth Bulletin* is published bi-monthly, also edited by McGavran. Church growth has even become an academic discipline: one can now earn an accredited M.A. in the field. It has almost gained the status of a science, having developed a specialized vocabulary and research method. Church growth studies of specific areas, mostly produced by those who have been included in the group of fifty-some career missionaries who enroll yearly in the Fuller Seminary course, are being published at the rate of several a year. Regions such as Jamaica, Mexico, Brazil, Nigeria, Korea, Tabasco, Liberia, and Latin America have been the subjects of published studies.

An article of McGavran's called "Wrong Strategy: The Real Crisis in Missions" was published in the *International Review of Missions* in 1965, and was considered so important for the present-day missionary enterprise that the 1968 issue for not being able to understand church growth. This, "con." McGavran admits he was not prepared for such a negative reaction. "I was surprised at the depth and thrust of the anti-church growth sentiment in several of them," he says. "Their authors may have been reacting excessively . . . . Such critical responses validate my thesis that mission strategies of the fifties and sixties were notably lacking in growth emphasis. Those who hold the current wrong strategy might have been expected to react vigorously to a dispassionate description of it."[1]

Church growth, negative and positive, has exerted a strong influence on Latin American Protestantism, and this is the reason for writing this brief chapter. The representatives of the radical left whom we have been investigating, along with others, have been quite outspoken in their criticism of the thesis that "what the world needs is not 'more of everything, whether churches multiply or not.' What the fantastically mounting population of this world needs is fantastically multiplying churches."[2]

In Latin America, as in other parts of the world, those who hold to a theology of presence, those who are clustered around what we have called the "passive pole of missions," are generally reluctant to dedicate themselves to produce vigorously growing churches. There are several reasons why Christians oppose church growth principles.

For some who are not always open to change, the newness of the idea is in itself a stumbling block. They are conservative. They say, "Modern missions have been operating well for 150 years, and we are satisfied with them today."

Others are simply ignorant. Up to recently few books have been written on the subject, curricula of seminaries and Bible institutes have not included church growth, and few mission leaders have attempted to build their strategy around it. Many of the ignorant warmly embrace church growth principles once they become informed.

Still others are bound by cultural overhang. They were born and brought up in lethargic, content, comfortable, and slowly growing churches in Eurica (the church growth abbreviation for the "sending countries"), and have not adequately made the cultural adjustment of Africasia ("the mission fields"), where often conditions favorable to rapid church growth are prevalent.

Ecclesiastical myopia may be another unsuspecting cause

mentioned above carried ten reactions to it, most of them for example, may be one reason why Dominican Father Jordan Bishop of Bolivia "does not share Donald McGavran's views as to the correct strategy for Christian mission."[3] Bishop's orientation is within Latin American Catholicism, which for centuries dominated a continent's religion by force. This was the Inquisition type of growth, which perhaps causes him to say, rightly, "We do not want church growth based on human power and prestige."[4] It is Bishop's conclusion that "In some situations a too-rapid numerical growth could create serious problems with respect both to the authenticity of Christianity and the future development of the Church in a given area."[5]

But there are more serious reasons for opposing church growth. One is psychological. A Christian worker finds himself in a situation where his church is not growing. It was not growing when he arrived, and the results did not improve no matter what he tried. He may have been brought up in a retarded church also. In seminary his professors did not teach him how to diagnose the health of a church and how to prescribe remedies that would either cure the disease or enable him to pronounce it chronic. He does not even know whether his church *can* grow. At that point he begins to rationalize, searching for something in the church he can call good, deciding that God is interested in quality rather than quantity, redefining such terms as "mission," "evangelism," "reconciliation," or "conversion," and eliminating others such as "saving souls," "new birth," or "eternal damnation." The rationalization thus deeply affects the way he reads his Bible or formulates his theological propositions. Finding little satisfaction in throwing himself entirely into unfruitful evangelism or church extension, he looks for another exciting cause, such as the revolution, into which he can divert his energies. Since he remains a pastor or Christian worker, he feels a special burden to relate his two callings in Christian and theological terminology.

This phenomenon in Latin America has occurred mostly in the churches of the older denominations. Gonzálo Castillo sums up the condition of these churches when he says:

> . . . both Catholicism and Protestantism find themselves unable to evangelize the Latin American man. In the case of Protestantism, this is all the more pronounced among the older denominations. In spite of certain reports of advance in evangelism,

the facts indicate that we have arrived at a point of stagnation and crisis . . . the youth decline to collaborate with their elders in a work which appears to them to be innocuous.[6]

It is not strange, therefore, that most of what we have called the psychological opposition to church growth originates with persons from the older denominations, not so much from those of the faith missions, the newer denominations, or the Pentecostal wing.

The second, more serious, reason for opposing church growth is theological. A secularized theology usually leads to a denial of evangelism as the primary function of the church in the world, and often to questioning the very validity of the church at all. Only on rare occasions in reading the literature of the Latin American radical left does one come across refreshing passages such as one written by Juan Tron and Antonio Cesari in a book published by the *Centro de Estudios*. They say that evangelism involves not only proclaiming Christ to individuals and communities, but also a response to this form of conversion and incorporation into the church through baptism. "Where any one of these elements lacks," they say, "the evangelistic work is incomplete."[7]

José Míguez Bonino, the scholarly moderate, also has written in favor of church growth. He says:

> . . . it is the work of God that causes growth, certifying in this way the apostolic preaching, bestowing His approval . . . . Preaching "with power" (with the Spirit) is often mentioned. . . . In this context, numbers manifest the grace of the Lord, His favor toward man.[8]

If this type of emphasis were more prevalent among those of the left, theological tensions among Protestants in Latin America would be reduced to a minimum, as they were a generation ago. But unhappily others take a rather harsh stand on the opposite side.

Carlos Valle, a Methodist from Argentina, in a Continental Consultation on Evangelism, says bluntly: "The mission of the Church is to evangelize . . . (but) to evangelize is not to convert, it is not to win souls to Christ, it is not to get members for the Church." "Evangelization," he went on, "doesn't refer particularly to individual souls, but rather to the definitive action of God in Jesus Christ to bring all the structures of this world toward their ultimate goal."[9]

Another Argentine Methodist pastor, Roberto Ríos, mentions the traditional concepts of evangelism by saying, "Among ourselves the mission of the Church consists in growing. Our congregational structures are based on the supposition that it is possible to measure the results of mission." But then he argues that this type of thinking is the "neuralgic point" in the River Plate area. He doubts that we can take it for granted if the church's mission is to bring more people into the congregation. This strong statement follows:

> Growth at all costs results not so much in the incorporation of souls into the Church as it does in a process of mass vaccination against the Gospel . . . . It produces a kind of reaction, the formation of antibodies against a Gospel which has been received in minimal doses.[10]

Of the theologians we have previously mentioned, Emilio Castro develops his doubts about church growth at the greatest length, calling it disdainfully "the modern agitation for statistics and numerical growth."[11] He feels that the "greatest obstacle to evangelization is the church that is preoccupied with its own existence."[12] "We should forget ourselves as institutions, and the preservation of our own existence," he suggests, "and seek the will of our Lord in Latin America."[13] In his most extensive passage, he ameliorates the blow somewhat by saying, "In no way do we want to look down upon the numerical growth of the Church . . . . " Then he writes:

> But we cannot ignore that *to the degree* that the numerical growth of the Church occupies the center of our attention, we slip away from the Gospel; we tend to oversimplify it, to reduce its demands, and to withdraw from real life. We walk through the world as if on a commando attack, looking for someone to capture so we can take him back to our church as a prisoner. We try to make sure that a good number of souls will have a comfortable place in eternity.[14]

This mockery of the soul-saving ministry of the church, held dear by a large majority of Latin American Protestants, does not help the image of the radical left among conservative evangelicals. Some of those on the left do not care. Although in a slightly different context, a group of them recently wrote concerning the Facultad Evangélica de Teología of Buenos Aires: "Its ecumenical commitment — although tending to estrange certain conservative evangelicals — has made possible a dialogue with the progressive, post-conciliar sectors of the Roman Catholic Church."[15]

One of Castro's basic errors, at least from the church growth point of view, is the distinction he attempts to make between church growth and faithfulness to God. He says that Paul "at no time established numerical growth as a goal of the Church," but rather his goal is "faithfulness to Christ crucified."[16] The following statement clarifies his position further:

> Faithfulness to the Gospel is more important than its propagation, and faithfulness and propagation are not always synonymous.[17]

This could scarcely be more opposed to McGavran's views. In a section entitled "Church Growth Is Faithfulness to God," McGavran says:

> Anyone who would comprehend the growth of Christian Churches must see it primarily as faithfulness to God. God desires it. The Christian, like his Master, is sent to seek and save the lost.[18]

The attempt on the part of the radical left to reduce the significance of church growth as a part of the total mission of the church can be ascribed to some extent to their disillusionment with conservatives who claim that church growth is *everything*. To make church growth the exclusive goal of the church in the world is as wrong as making social service the exclusive goal. Here the choice is not between good and evil, but in the familiar terms of the Sears Roebuck catalog: good, better, and best. The New Testament commands us to win souls and it commands us to love our neighbor. What we are here discussing is basically a matter of priority.

All of what the church does in the world — building schools and hospitals, dialoguing with non-Christians, joining civil rights marches, lobbying in congress, bandaging the sores of lepers, teaching peasants how to grow bigger crops, distributing contraceptives — all these are good, and if

Christians feel led to do this they should receive all possible encouragement. But the error is to describe these activities as "mission" to the exclusion of church growth or just to add church growth to the long list of other good things the church should do in the world.

McGavran believes that the type of left-wing strategy we have been describing is "really a defense of the existing machine of mission, its departments, vested interests, bureaucracies and massive service arms." He objects to slogans such as "the whole Gospel," designed to cloud the real issue. He says that:

> The issue is whether the apostles shall wait on tables. The issue is whether Paul at Troas hearing, "Come over to Macedonia and help us," shall send over some specialists to enter into dialogue with the priests of Jove and Venus, and others assist a revolt against Roman oppression and slave-holding. The issue is that, while we proclaim "the whole Gospel" to "the whole man," opportunities for propagating the Christian religion are neglected.[19]

A series of lectures given in Bolivia by J. G. Davies of Birmingham University have now been published in Spanish under the title *Diálogo con el mundo (Dialogue with the World)*. Davies was also perhaps McGavran's harshest critic in the issue of *International Review of Missions* mentioned at the beginning of this chapter. He argues that the church growth point of view tends to "reduce the living God of radical monotheism to a tribal deity."[20] He does not believe that Christians should indulge in "the intent to extend the Church."[21] "We must recognize that to consider establishing the Church as the foremost Christian activity is absurd," he writes.[22] A master of barbed phrases, Davies declares himself against "the vicious circle which begins with the Church and ends with the Church, which is to convert ecclesiology into ecclesiolatry."[23] He would like to see "the word conversion eliminated from Christian vocabulary."[24] He feels that the world should give the agenda to the church and that Christians should be concerned with dialogue, not with church extension.

The last words spoken by Christ while on this earth cannot be taken lightly. To "go," to "make disciples," to "baptize them," and to "teach them all things," must be our first priority if we are to be faithful to God. To do the good and the better is a virtue. But to neglect the best is sin. The angels in heaven rejoice when one sinner comes to repentance. This is church growth, and this is the characteristic view of today's Latin American Protestantism.

NOTES TO CHAPTER 3

1. Donald A. McGavran, "Church Growth Strategy Continued," *International Review of Missions*, LVII, 227 (July, 1968), p. 336.
2. Donald A. McGavran, "Wrong Strategy: The Real Crisis in Missions," *International Review of Missions*, LIV, 216 (October, 1965), p. 457.
3. Jordan Bishop, O. P., "Numerical Growth — an Adequate Criterion of Mission?" *International Review of Missions*, LVII, 227 (July, 1968), p. 290.
4. *Ibid.*, p. 289.
5. *Ibid.*, p. 287.
6. Gonzálo Castillo Cárdenas, "The Life and Witness of the Church in Latin America," *Witness in Six Continents* (1964), pp. 31-32.
7. Juan Tron and Antonio Cesari, "Evangelización, comunidad y proselytismo," *Polémica, Diálogo y Misión*, José Míguez Bonino, ed. (1966), p. 50.
8. José Míguez Bonino, "Un Dios que actúa y renueva la iglesia," *América Hoy* (1966), p. 41.
9. Carlos Valle, "Presuposiciones teológicas de la evangelización" (1966), pp. 1-2.
10. Roberto Ríos, "¿Qué estructuras de las congregaciones locales impiden la obra misionera?" *Cuadernos Teológicos*, XIII, 3 (julio-septiembre, 1964), p. 89.
11. Emilio Castro, *Misión, presencia y diálogo* (1964), p. 11.
12. Emilio Castro, "Evangelization in Latin America," *International Review of Missions*, LIII, 212 (October, 1964), p. 452.
13. *Ibid.*, p. 453.
14. Emilio Castro, "Misión y evangelización," *Id por el mundo* (1966), p. 17.
15. Ricardo Chartier, *et al.*, "Missionary Structures and Training for Mission — The River Plate Area," *International Review of Missions*, LVII, 226 (April, 1968), p. 219.
16. Castro, "Misión y evangelización," p. 18.
17. Castro, "Evangelization in Latin America," p. 453.
18. Donald A. McGavran, *Understanding Church Growth*, p. 15.
19. McGavran, "Wrong Strategy: The Real Crisis in Missions," p. 454.
20. J. G. Davies, "Church Growth: A Critique," *International Review of Missions*, LVII, 227 (July, 1968), p. 291.
21. J. G. Davies, *Diálogo con el mundo* (1967), p. 49.
22. *Ibid.*, p. 50.
23. *Ibid.*, p. 52.
24. *Ibid.*, p. 67.

Chapter 4

RADICAL THEOLOGY AS SYNCRETISM

One of the major study topics of the Congress on the Church's Worldwide Mission held at Wheaton, Illinois, in 1966, was syncretism. While the Congress itself dealt primarily with the theoretical aspects of syncretism, it did recommend that evangelicals in all parts of the world study the syncretistic tendencies in their specific areas and inform their colleagues as to the results. The text of the Wheaton Declaration is as follows:

> We therefore declare that, while seeking greater effectiveness in the communication of the Christian faith and acknowledging the uniqueness and finality of Jesus Christ, we will expose the dangers of syncretism . . . we will acquaint our total leadership more carefully with the religious beliefs and thought-forms of the peoples among whom they live and serve, relative to syncretistic tendencies.[1]

The purpose of this chapter is to raise the question of the possibility of syncretism in the Latin American radical left.

Commonly, syncretism in Latin America does not conjure up images of well-dressed, cultured, and highly educated preachers in affluent city churches. Most would think of it in terms of a Guatemalan Indian sacrificing a chicken on the steps of a Roman Catholic cathedral, or a darkened room in a Sao Paulo *favela* where a medium chants mumbo-jumbo to the spirits of the dead while wearing a crucifix around her neck. Undoubtedly the Christo-paganism, which has resulted from the adoption of Catholic forms and the retention of animistic content since the days of the Spanish conquest, involves more Latin Americans in syncretism than does any other religious expression. Brazilian Spiritism and Haitian Voodooism would run a close second, and this type of syncretism also merits close investigation. Many erroneously feel that they can be good Catholics and good Spiritists at the same time.

The new radical left in Latin America does not involve nearly the number of people that the more popular forms of syncretism do, but its potential influence on the Protestant community is ominous. At this point it would be easy either to stack the cards or beg the question. No one likes to be involved in syncretism, and the term has taken on negative implications. Since it is almost an insult, mentioning names here would be ungracious, so we will attempt to stick to general ideas, recognizing the accompanying risk of oversimplification. Since part of the motivation for this study came from the Wheaton Congress, perhaps the best starting point would be the definition of syncretism used in the Wheaton Declaration:

> Syncretism, for our purposes, is the attempt to unite or reconcile Biblically-revealed Christian truth with the diverse or opposing tenets and practices of non-Christian religions or other systems of thought that deny it.[2]

In the preliminary study paper of the Wheaton Congress, Jack Shepherd discerned three specific types of syncretism. He classified them as follows:

> (1) *Assimilative syncretism* incorporates elements of non-Christian religions, assuming there is no qualitative difference between the Christian and other faiths.
> (2) *Syncretism by accommodation* reduces or rephrases the Gospel message. It develops as a result of un-Biblical naturalistic thought in one's interpretation of Christian truth.
> (3) *Syncretism through accretions* in which secondary beliefs and practices overlap and obscure the basic message.[3]

Assimilative syncretism involves an interaction with non-Christian religions. It implies the effort described by Visser 't Hooft as the attempt "to harmonize as much as possible all religious ideas and experiences so as to create one universal religion for mankind."[4] While this type of syncretism might apply to Latin American Christo-paganism, the new radical left is not making any attempt to join with non-Christian faiths.

Syncretism through accretions obviously is directed toward some of the more fundamentalistic tendencies to set higher requirements for salvation than either God or the Bible does. But here the basic message of Christianity is not involved per se. The new radical left is highly critical of "pietism" and undoubtedly could point to specific instances of syncretistic accretions in the mainstream of Latin American Protestantism. It should be noted, however, that the final Wheaton Declaration does not mention this rather novel proposal, although evangelicals would do well to be sensitive to its implications. In any case, the radical left is more in danger of altering the core than adding to it.

The syncretism that poses a danger to Latin American Protestantism is, therefore, *syncretism by accommodation*. In the attempt to make the Christian message relevant to a society caught in the throes of rapid social change, some of the representatives of this group go so far in their reduction and rephrasing of the message that they end up with "another gospel," to use Paul's phrase of Galatians 1:8-9. In its extreme forms it represents a capitulation of Christianity to secularism.

Naturally, all the representatives of the Latin American radical left whose viewpoints we have discussed in Chapter 2 would not be guilty of syncretism. The majority, in fact, would not. It seems that some, however, tend toward syncretism, and a warning should be raised. The more radical of the leftist theologians are the vanguard. Ideas they expressed ten years ago were considered far out, but today they have a much wider acceptance among the liberally-oriented segment of Latin American Protestantism. Some, as a matter of fact, are now almost axiomatic, such as "cosmic redemption," "social reconciliation," and "the extension of the incarnation." While these ideas have been pouring out for the past few years in prestigious Latin American journals such as *Cuadernos Teológicos* (now extinct) and *Cristianismo y sociedad,* very little has been written by evangelicals in Spanish to analyze these views and present evangelical alternatives. This is a situation that must be corrected at once. Perhaps the Latin American delegates to the Congresses of Wheaton and Berlin in 1966 or those who will attend the Latin American Congress on Evangelism in Bogotá in 1969 will shoulder more responsibility in the future.

There is little doubt that the most radical expressions of this liberal theology fall into the category of syncretism by accommodation. Their exponents will deny this, naturally. All think they are preaching the pure Biblical Gospel. Unfortunately, they are not. They are involved in the dangerous paradox of going forth as Christians but preaching "another gospel." Secularism has swept over the world like a vicious sandstorm, attempting to make a spiritual desert of our planet.

The Chilean Pentecostals, famous as one of Latin America's most vigorous, fast-growing, and completely indigenous groups, have seen the picture clearly. They use a slightly different analogy:

> The large painting which adorns Pentecostal sanctuaries depicts a restless sea surrounding an island upon the rocks of which a Bible lies open, illuminated by a ray of light from heaven. . . . The symbolism is obvious. In a deeply evil world of misery and perdition, the Christian communities stand like islands of peace and repose. The task of the elect is to give refuge to the drowning, without a thought for how the angry sea might be calmed.[5]

While it might be exaggerating somewhat to say that there is "no thought" as to how to still the sea, or that Chilean Pentecostals are on a "social strike," as Lalive says in another place,[6] the emphasis on the compelling need to rescue the drowning is accurate. This is one reason why the churches are growing so rapidly.

Attempting to stop the sandstorm or calm the waves, as the church's *primary mission* in the world, is the "other gospel." *Those theologians who feel that proclaiming salvation, persuading men and women to become Christ's disciples, baptizing them, and building the church is either irrelevant, superfluous, peripheral, or even secondary to the social ministry of the church in the world are guilty of reconciling Biblically revealed Christian truth with the diverse and opposing tenets of secularism, which according to our definition is syncretism by accommodation.*

Although he naturally does not look at the problem from the same perspective, Peter Berger, President of the Society for the Scientific Study of Religion, makes a fascinating analysis of the process we have been calling "syncretism by accommodation," under the title "A Sociological View of the Secularization of Theology." Our contention has been that, in many cases, representatives of the Latin American radical left begin with a priori socio-economic-political viewpoints and formulate a theology that will support these. Berger agrees that secular theology is an accommodation to sociological presuppositions, some of which cannot be substantiated. He says:

> The sociologically derived programs for theology and church give cognitive as well as practical priority to the reality presuppositions of the man in the street over those of the religious tradition.[7]

Berger charges that the secular theologians' reinterpretation of the Christian tradition "entails an accommodation between the tradition and what is, correctly or not, taken to be modern consciousness."[8] This process is what we feel involves a syncretistic tendency, because where there is a question as to which of the two emphases will give way when a conflict arises, "almost invariably the religious tradition is made to conform to the cognitive and normative standard of the alleged modern consciousness."[9] Berger questions whether the secular theologians have even accurately evaluated modern ideas. He points out how risky it is to relativize theology on that basis once the ideas themselves can be relativized.

The secular theologians have already gone so far, in Berger's opinion, that the only thing left is "the final self-liquidation of the ecclesiastical-theological enterprise as such."[10] Of course, as we have seen, some of the Latin American theologians would not mourn if this happened. Berger thinks that "accommodation with the secular theologians has become total." He concludes with a rather humorous analogy:

> The whole thing reminds one strongly of the old story of the drunkard who carefully walked in the gutter so that he could not possibly fall into it. The transformation of transcendence into immanence and the change from objectivity to subjectivity, is completed. The paradoxical result is that one can now feel safe from the secularizing and subjectivizing forces threatening the tradition. The worst, so to speak, has already happened — one has pre-empted it to oneself.[11]

Thus, the extreme segment of the Latin American radical left is susceptible to charges of syncretism from two points of view. First, by allowing other good but secondary functions of the church to usurp the first priority of aggressive, church-building evangelism. Secondly, by allowing theological considerations to be molded by relative and passing sociological factors rather than beginning with and building on the objective revelation of God in His Word. Accommodation to the "reality presuppositions of our age"[12] is nothing less than devastating to Christian theology.

One always runs a risk in making such a strong statement. It might leave the impression that one is against social action as a legitimate function of the church. I assuredly am not. Christians cannot love their neighbors as themselves without doing something about the social needs around them. They cannot play the role of the priest and Levite on the Jericho Road. Each Christian must be a good Samaritan, ready to pour oil into the wounds of his neighbor who is downtrodden, and even to take necessary steps to correct the social ills that cause him to be downtrodden. These are good and necessary objectives and will be developed in Chapter 6. Only if they obscure or dilute the principal evangelistic function of the church do they become evil.

NOTES TO CHAPTER 4

1. Harold Lindsell, ed., *The Church's Worldwide Mission* (1966), p. 223.

2. *Ibid.*, p. 22.

3. Jack F. Shepherd, "Mission — and Syncretism," *The Church's Worldwide Mission* (1966), p. 86.

4. W. A. Visser 't Hooft, *No Other Name: The Choice Between Syncretism and Christian Universalism* (1963), p. 11.

5. Christian Lalive, "The Pentecostal 'Conquista' in Chile," *The Ecumenical Review* (January, 1968), p. 24.

6. Christian Lalive, *El refugio de las masas: estudio sociológico del protestantismo chileno* (1968).

7. Peter Berger, "A Sociological View of the Secularization of Theology," *Journal for the Scientific Study of Religion* (Spring, 1967), p. 7.

8. *Ibid.*

9. *Ibid.*, p. 9.

10. *Ibid.*, p. 14.

11. *Ibid.*

12. *Ibid.*

Chapter 5

EVANGELICAL ALTERNATIVES

When one begins to gather the writings of the Latin American conservative evangelical theologians, he soon comes almost to despair. The vast amount of literature that is emerging from the pens and presses of the radical left is overwhelming when placed alongside the scanty offerings of the evangelicals.

While this is in one sense a lamentable situation, it is not beyond understanding. Evangelicals through the past few decades have been about what they have considered "their Father's business" — that of preaching the Gospel. Little time has been dedicated to reflection and writing. They belong to the "active," not the "passive" pole. In analyzing the situation, three positive factors combine to explain, at least in part, the relative lack of theological expression on the part of Latin American evangelicals.

The Bible-school orientation of many of the pioneers among the evangelical missionaries is one factor. Trained in the pre-World War II era, they lived through the period when seminary after seminary fell into the liberal camp, and when God was raising up evangelical Bible institutes to take their places. The word "seminary" to many conjured up the image of an institution of destruction. Nor only were they disinclined to create similar institutions on the mission field, but with only Bible-school diplomas, they would not have been qualified to teach on the seminary level even if they had created them. This lack of seminaries consequently did not encourage gifted young men to move into the academic pursuits that would have been necessary for an important theological production in their generation.

The spirit of separatism in many of the early evangelical workers also was a detriment to serious theological production. The separatism referred to here is not separatism from the world, the flesh, and the devil so much as an isolation from the opposing theological currents. Libraries in many of the Bible schools refused to catalog "questionable" books. Students were taught the dangers of modernism, but they were seldom allowed to capture the thought processes of the men who were teaching it. Secondary sources were relied upon, and the students had little possible way of checking them against primary sources, nor were they encouraged to do so. This somewhat nervous type of pedagogy stifled many aspirations to higher scholarship before they were able to get a good start.

The third negative factor was a clear anti-intellectualism on the part of some. Perhaps the Chilean Pentecostals have provided the most obvious example of this tendency. None of the hundreds of pastors in the larger Pentecostal denominations is a graduate of a seminary or Bible institute. The apprentice system they practice trains ministers, but bypasses institutions. It is, as Christian Lalive says, "education in the street."[1] Whereas this system has helped to produce some of the most vigorously growing churches in the whole world, needless to say it has not produced high-level theologians.

Switching to a more positive point of view, we could say that another factor that has influenced the evangelical wing of the church has been an overriding sense of evangelistic imperative. Systematic theology is not necessary to preach the Gospel and win souls to Christ. Theological formation demands a certain detachment, blocks of time for meditation and study, and a sense of objectivity. Evangelistic passion, especially where results are seen on every hand, demands involvement, activity, and a sacrificial program of person-to-person encounter. In the context of a rapidly growing church, theological pursuits are considered a luxury.

When church and mission are evangelistically-oriented, theological education is geared toward the training of evangelists to win souls and plant churches, and pastors to feed the flock. In the conservative evangelical camp, funds for scholarships for higher education are difficult to come by. The gifted evangelical who is able to study at higher levels abroad is the exception, but it will be noticed that without exception the men who are becoming known in Latin America as theologians have taken studies outside of Latin America.

The final factor that perhaps has prevented evangelicals from entering more fully into the theological debate has been a disinterestedness. The radical left, regardless of the books they publish, the trips they make around the continent, or the well-publicized "encounters" they hold, really constitute a small minority of Latin American Protestants. I have heard estimates of 1 to 5 percent, rarely more. Many evangelicals disdainfully ask: Are they worth answering?

Four representative Latins have been chosen as examples of evangelical theological thinking in Latin America. None of these four men, nor any other Latin American who is identified with the evangelical wing of the church, has a theological work listed in John Sinclair's *Protestantism in Latin America: A Bibliographical Guide*,[2] the definitive work on the subject to date. This is not because Sinclair was biased, but rather because these writings are virtually nonexistent.

Neither Vangioni, Padilla, Rico, nor Fajardo has written a book on theology. Some Latin Americans have written theologically-oriented books, but they have either been anti-Catholic polemics or restatements of the traditional evangelical corpus of "systematic theology." Rarely even in an article can one find an evangelical leader who has entered into the dialogue of the day and said something significant about the relationship of the church to the contemporary world.

The reason for the choice of these four is simply that they have been aware enough of theological currents in Latin America to address themselves at least once to the issues. The Berlin Congress on Evangelism played a very significant role in bringing this about. The core material from Vangioni, Rico, and Fajardo was drawn from their addresses in Berlin. If it had not been for that stimulus, this chapter probably could not have been written. As it is, the sparseness of the source material and the superficiality of the theological development make the position of these men disproportionately vulnerable to attacks from the radical theologians.

Vangioni, Padilla, and Rico all place the social responsibility of the church in such a low-priority category that social service would hardly qualify as a legitimate Christian activity. There is little question that this negative attitude accurately reflects the mentality of the great majority of Latin American evangelicals, and it manifests itself in the fact that a large part of Protestant social work in Latin America has gone into the hands of the liberal wing of the church by default. Happily, this attitude is undergoing some change in many circles, and evangelicals are recognizing that it is pleasing to God not only to win a soul but to give a glass of cold water in the name of Christ. It is hoped that the final chapter of this book will be helpful in establishing this principle on a Biblical basis.

Fajardo is a step ahead of many Latin American evangelicals when he recognizes social service as having intrinsic value. His written theological development is still in the embryonic stage, however, and needs further expression.

It is embarrassing to have to use the Evangelism in Depth school as the final theological position of evangelicals because its theology has largely been developed by non-Latin Americans such as Kenneth Strachan, Horace Fenton, and Dayton Roberts. Rubén Lores has done some writing on the theological aspects of Evangelism in Depth, but it is symptomatic that his writings were not well enough known to come to Sinclair's attention and be included in his *Bibliography*.

One of the curious aspects of the evangelical segment of the Latin American church has been a rather strongly negative attitude to theology in general, especially when applied to the contemporary scene. Many have a deep feeling that theology is an American, British, or German import that can easily be done without. Some are expecting that an ethereal "Latin American theology" will somehow develop without reference to the theological currents in other parts of the world. When the modern theological dialogue is mentioned, some react by saying, "This is just another tactic of foreign imperialists to try to divide Latin American Protestants." I asked a delegate returning from the Berlin Congress, effervescent from his journey, what the principal theological issues were. "Oh," he replied, "very little theology was mentioned. It was a congress for *evangelization*."

With all its weaknesses in articulation, however, evangelical theology has been operative in Latin America. As one leader recently said, "It is difficult to find our declared fundamental theology. It just hasn't been said. Thank God it has been practiced, however, and that voices are beginning to be prepared who can define our theology."

Fernando Vangioni: "The Divine Dynamic"

Argentine Fernando Vangioni was the only Latin American among the eight who delivered "main addresses" at the World

Congress on Evangelism held in Berlin in 1966. He is known in virtually every Latin American republic for his outstanding gift of evangelism. For years he has been associated with the Latin American Billy Graham team.

Vangioni's burden at Berlin was that Christians world-around recover the apostolic dynamic. "Every preacher," he said, should "aspire to be filled with the Holy Ghost."[3] The Gospel is nothing, if it is not preached with this supernatural power. Faith in Christ is the all-important solution to man's deepest needs, and "Only the Word of God . . . can pierce the soul and disarm man's rational intentions and create faith."[4] Vangioni, then, introduces a supernatural dimension that we have not found to be prominent in the radical left.

While Vangioni does not ignore man's socio-economic-political problems, he feels that prior to seeking solutions to those problems, man's need of "reconciliation with the Father, forgiveness of sins, and peace of soul"[5] must be met. He is primarily concerned with "man's lost condition, his spiritual ruin, and separation from God." Reconciliation for Vangioni is vertical, not horizontal.

The eschatological urgency of preaching the Gospel is evident in the writings of the evangelicals. As Efraín Santiago, also until recently associated with Billy Graham, says:

> To be free from the blood of all men we must pray, we must send, we must go, we must mobilize every soldier, we must use every modern method, and we must win! It is either heaven or hell for the ninety and nine that are lost. They must hear God's word.[6]

Vangioni expresses a similar concern. "Those whose names are not written in the Book of Life, says God's Word, will be cast into the lake of fire; this is the second death."[7] This emphasis has virtually disappeared from the theology of the radical left. Teaching about hell seems to them to be either antiquated or erroneous. Evangelical theology is in strong disagreement with the incipient universalism noticed in some of the secular theologians.

Vangioni looks forward to a day when human problems will be solved. He is aware that

> There have never been so many destroyed homes, so many broken hearts, so many young people drifting as slaves to vice

85

and sin, so much corruption, crime and hate, so much international unrest, so many social problems.[8]

But Vangioni, with the evangelical version of the "theology of hope," awaits "a future day when all human problems will be forever ended, sin will have been removed from the earth, and death will be no more."[9]

How will this day come? Vangioni is convinced that it "will not come through the efforts of men or nations."[10] He does not believe that the resources of Christians spent on the attempt to bring about, through human efforts, the end of the miseries of mankind, are well-invested. The "sublime ending to the story of man's miserable and sad history" will come only through the supernatural intervention of God.

Vangioni expresses his conviction that a gospel without the Biblical basis or without the cross of Christ presents a danger to the Christian cause in Latin America. Without using the term, he refers to what we have called the theology of the radical left in these words:

> Such a message pretends to be modern by adapting itself to the spirit of the times, to a mentality that has departed from the divine purpose both in language and in spirit; although pretending to fill a present need, it has lost authority and spiritual power, influence and impact on lives and hearts. It is an empty, hollow message, the product of a sophisticated age; while professing to be relevant, it cannot be, because the deep problems, the acute crisis, the incurable ills and desperate spiritual state of humanity cry out for and require the true word of the Gospel.[11]

The divine dynamic of the Gospel can solve the problems of man, Vangioni preaches. "Only the Gospel has the solution for so much evil, the answer to many questions, for only the Lord Jesus Christ, the Desire of all nations, can put an end to this tragic state of affairs."[12]

Washington Padilla: "Not by Bread Alone"

Ecuador's Washington Padilla has frequently addressed himself to the social problems of Latin America in relationship to the Gospel. He is acutely aware that man is not just a spiritual being, and that Christianity must take into consideration other needs as well. He says, for example:

86

Man's physical needs are something which Christianity, following the example of her Founder, fully recognizes, preaching that to deprive a man of material means is criminal and against all principles of humanity and justice.[13]

The problem in much of Latin America, however, is not recognizing the physical and material side of man's being, but to be caught by the fallacy that this is all of man. "The whole world seems to be completely given over to the mad race for a better physical life,"[14] Padilla says. No one denies the importance of food, clothing, and shelter, but "the economic and material needs of man are not everything: they are part of life, and a tremendously important part; but there are spiritual needs which must be equally satisfied."[15]

Padilla bases this concept on the fact that man is made in the image of God. This raises his spiritual stature much above his physical in ultimate importance. The spirit of man needs attention. "It must be cultivated, it must be developed, it must be molded, it must be led," Padilla says.[16] To neglect this aspect of man is superficial — one never arrives at the root of the problem.

Social problems must be seen in this light, according to Padilla. He is disturbed because

> The social "physicians" prescribe all kinds of remedies according to their particular ideologies, all attempting to cure the ills that are hindering the progress of our peoples through social legislation, economic restructuring, and political reform.[17]

This type of social action, however, often is mistaken because it "leaves out the most important factor, the factor that all peoples have in common: the human factor."[18]

If the man who forms the building block of society is not changed, it is impossible to build a sound society. "All efforts to construct a better society with ethically deficient men are doomed to failure," Padilla says.[19] In order to solve our social problems we will have to find better material than we have now. Man can, and should, be changed. Padilla states:

> We must never forget that for an economic, political, or social system to succeed, first and foremost the *man* must be changed, his human nature must be transformed, his selfishness, ambition, injustice, phoniness, and cruelty must be re-

placed by the moral and spiritual virtues that constitute the very base of human life. On such foundations those socio-economic-political systems can be constructed.[20]

This man-in-society can be changed only by Christ. Therefore the personal relationship of each individual with Jesus Christ is the all-important key. The type of evangelism that sees as its result transformed lives is "the prior condition which we need to fulfill if we ever want to see our people moving toward a better future."[21] Padilla's conclusion sounds almost like an invitation at the end of an evangelistic sermon:

> Only when we, the inhabitants of this great continent, surrender to the transforming power of Jesus Christ will we lay the solid moral foundations of all social well-being.[22]

José María Rico: "Social Renewal Through New Birth"

The conversion of Father José María Rico in Bolivia in 1956 was an event that shook Bolivian Catholicism severely, and encouraged Bolivian Protestants with the reminder of the regenerating power of the Holy Spirit.[23] Ever since, both in his ministry in association with the Andes Evangelical Mission and subsequently as an international evangelist with the Assemblies of God, Rico has had an ever widening influence throughout Latin America. He preaches the new birth because he has personally experienced it so deeply. He now represents the Pentecostal wing of the church, although his theological training naturally was not within the Pentecostal orbit. Born in Spain, he is a naturalized Bolivian citizen.

Rico is one of the few Latin American evangelicals who have made an attempt to develop a theology of the relation of the church to the world, and in doing so face radical theology squarely. His theological position, although not shared in detail by all evangelicals, is typical of a large segment of those who hold the more conservative social views.

Rico would "commend efforts that result in benefit to society,"[24] but he is highly suspicious of dedicating church resources and programs toward that end. In the first place, these social activities cannot be considered as efficacious in the salvation of men. In the second place, the Bible says to seek first the Kingdom of God and then worry about the additions. But he criticizes the radical theologians (referring to them slightly inaccurately as teaching the "social gospel") because

> They spend all their energy, time and money in search of the "additions" but they do not have a free minute to lead men to God. They are so socially and politically occupied that they spend their lives trying to increase their influence in society without realizing that their faith, piety, and love gradually change into a simple act of philanthropy, which has no supernatural value whatsoever in the eyes of God.[25]

The concept, common among secular theologians, that "man is just one of many cells in a collective social group"[26] does not impress Rico. He insists that the Gospel "focuses on the individual as the direct object of the entire divine plan."[27] Therefore the new birth of the individual is the all-important goal of the church. As he analyzes social needs he comes to the conclusion:

> What society needs, therefore, is the multiplication of these new creatures in its fold. When these take control of society, society will experience total and natural renewal.[28]

Taking the example of Jesus as his illustration, he says that He "never assumed attitudes which would have been favorable to those who preach the 'social gospel.' "[29] Jesus' land was under the unjust domination of the Roman forces when He lived His human life. The Romans were oppressors, and hated by the common man. Jesus could have risen to be a great *caudillo* in defense of the poor, the humble, and the dispossessed. But, Rico points out, "Christ never so much as made a single movement of rebellion against the Roman invaders."[30] He counseled His followers to render to Caesar what was Caesar's and to God what was God's.

Undoubtedly one of the most despised social injustices of the first century was the institution of slavery. Rico indicates that Christ could have defended those human beings whose liberty had been denied, but neither He nor His apostles took the road of "social action." Both Peter (1 Pet. 2:18) and Paul (Tit. 2:9) exhorted the slaves to obey their masters, not to seek freedom.

Rico's final illustration of our Lord's disengagement from the secular problems of His day is the episode in which some brothers came to Jesus asking Him to intervene in an economic injustice concerning their inheritance. Jesus answered, "Man, who made me a judge or divider over you?" (Luke 12:14). Rico's comment is:

> His mission was so distant from this type of problem that He did not want to set a precedent among His followers in matters touching human and material situations. Jesus' great social axiom is sufficiently clear in these words of His: "Seek ye first the kingdom of God and His righteousness, and all these things shall be added unto you."[31]

The "final conclusion" for Rico is that we must "preach the true Gospel of Christ." It is not just an option for the Christian, but an absolute necessity. "When we do this," Rico says, "a miracle will be produced that not even the best-intended socio-political effort could accomplish," for then "everything will be made new."[32]

José Fajardo: "The Banana-Halter Method"

In the World Congress on Evangelism in Berlin, Colombian educator José Fajardo addressed the assembly on "The Social Program of the Church." In this excellent message, he exhibited an evangelistic desire similar to that of the other representative evangelicals, but his theology differed in one important aspect. Fajardo set forth Christian social action as an end in itself, not as another evangelistic tool.

Fajardo objects to evangelicals who offer social service along with the insinuation that "we do what we do in order to get them into our churches and to take up our form of creed."[33] He suggests with a tone of accusation that this is the characteristic Western philosophy of social service in the Christian church. This hope, that those helped would follow us into our churches, he calls the "banana-halter" method. He says:

> When I was a child they used to send me out into the pasture to get a horse. I would carry a banana in one hand in front of me and the halter in the other hand behind me.[34]

He opposes using social service as a "banana."

Not that Fajardo is indifferent to individual salvation as

are some of the radical theologians. He explains it this way: "Naturally we want eventually to bring everyone to the feet of our Lord in order that they be saved, but even if those whom we serve should not accept Him as their Saviour, we should still continue to serve them, if they need our help."[35] This refreshing emphasis will be developed further in the following chapter, but in passing it would be well to note that many evangelicals do not agree that social service has intrinsic merit. Fajardo is aware of this, and in self-defense admits to his audience that his point of view "may sound heretical and even offensive."[36] It should not offend anyone, however. The Bible commands us to love our neighbor, and true love has no price tag. In loving our neighbor we are pleasing God.

This emphasis should not be confused with the teaching of radical theology. Fajardo sees this clearly. He criticizes missionaries he has heard say, "Do not preach a social gospel, because that will not save or change the people." It is true about the social gospel, but Fajardo points out that "social *service* need not be the 'social gospel.' "[37] He then defines social service:

> Social service really means actually doing things for people right where they are and where they need it. It means serving those that do not belong to our own denomination, or creed, or language, or race. It means doing something about their pain and suffering, for the sake of Christian love.[38]

The secular theologians will claim that no valuable social work can be accomplished if the social status quo is not overthrown by one means or another. They would criticize Fajardo's social program as superficial, and suggest that he become more revolutionary. But the program that Fajardo mentions does not need a revolution on the political scale to accomplish. It may well need a revolution in evangelical thinking. He proposes that the evangelical church show more of its love and concern for the world in areas of public health, urban problems, housing, sanitation, malnutrition, water supply, agriculture, protection of the rights of small businesses, orphanages, homes for the aged, and rehabilitation of social outcasts.

As the evangelical church becomes more involved in this kind of activity, Fajardo feels that one by-product will be a more willing ear on the part of the Latin Americans in general to the message they preach. Many Latin Americans are skeptical about Protestantism, and waiting to see what is its attitude toward the multitudes who are crying for help.

Fajardo concludes, "Could we not show these people that we are concerned not only for the salvation of their souls but also for all areas of their lives, a concern that may determine their attitude toward God?"[39] His plea deserves to be heard.

Evangelism in Depth: "Revolution in Evangelism"

Rarely, if ever, has an international, interdenominational effort made such an intense impact on the Latin American Protestant church as has the father of "saturation evangelism" movements, Evangelism in Depth. "Evangelismo a Fondo" has become such a household word to Latin American evangelicals that they at times expect to find it listed in their Bible concordances. Before mentioning the theological issues that Evangelism in Depth has raised, it would be well to say a word about the movement in general.

The late R. Kenneth Strachan, while Director of the Latin America Mission (1950-1965), made a special study of several growing movements, both Christian and non-Christian, in order to discover their secret of growth. His conclusion was summed up in what is now called the "Strachan theorem":

> The growth of any movement is in direct proportion to the success of that movement in mobilizing its total membership in the constant propagation of its beliefs.[40]

The Strachan theorem led its author to devise a year-long program that could be introduced into any country through its evangelical churches. Its basic thrust was to revive the church through prayer, train the Christian leaders who in turn would train or mobilize every member of their churches, then put this enlightened desire to win souls into practice through house-to-house visitation; special efforts for youth, women, children, university students, etc.; local, regional, and national campaigns; and a subsequent follow-up. Full-scale programs began in Nicaragua in 1960 and have since been held in Costa Rica, Guatemala, Honduras, Venezuela, Bolivia, Dominican Republic, Peru, Colombia, and Ecuador.

Over the past few years the Latin America Mission has made Evangelism in Depth its major sphere of activity. In public relations material Evangelism in Depth is often characterized as "revolutionary," which is a good term for almost anything in Latin America. The word "revolution" is right at home there. Almost every political slogan implies that its protagonists are in favor of revolution. Since Evangelism in Depth is to a large extent a native Latin American evangelistic movement, the slogan "Revolution in Evangelism," which is also the title of Dayton Roberts' study of the movement,[41] fits very nicely. John Stam of the Latin American Bible Seminary in Costa Rica characterizes Evangelism in Depth as a "theological revolution" also.[42] Roberts says that whereas Evangelism in Depth often has been described as primarily a method, there is no question that the method is based on important theological presuppositions.[43]

Stam explains that his use of "theological revolution" does not mean either that basic theology has changed, or that Evangelism in Depth takes sides on such debates as Calvinism vs. Arminianism, dispensationalism vs. Pentecostalism, etc. Evangelism in Depth, Stam says, is

> a different kind of theological revolution. Its objective is to make all theology revolutionary by locating doctrine within its original context of evangelism.[44]

This implies a focus on "total evangelism." It embraces the effect of the Gospel on every aspect of human life, and develops theology from that point of view.

Rubén Lores, who now heads up the Worldwide Office of Evangelism in Depth in Miami, has attempted a systematic exposition of Evangelism in Depth's theological position in a paper that has been published on several occasions, one of which was in a meeting of Lores with a group of radical theologians in Cochabamba, Bolivia, in 1966. In the paper he claims that "Evangelism in Depth is a practical expression of a theological reflection, confronted by the inescapable consideration of the mission of the church in this world."[45] The theology of Evangelism in Depth is a "hidden infrastructure" that undergirds its entire program.

Lores's starting point is the proclamation of the Gospel, which he considers to be the mission of the church. "This proclamation," he says, "is not a historical contingency; it is always a theological necessity."[46] He goes on to develop what he considers to be the five major theological emphases of Evangelism in Depth.

First, the Great Commission is imperative upon every Christian, not only upon the apostles. Second, success in evangelism resides, not in the Christians themselves, but in the power of Christ working through them. Third, the strategic objective of evangelism is to win nations by winning the individuals who make up the nations. Fourth, proclamation not only demands a decision, but also subsequent teaching so that converts continue on in their faith. Fifth, success in evangelization is to a degree proportionate to success in uniting the different members of the body of Christ in a given nation for a cooperative program.[47]

Whereas Lores's observations reflect standard evangelical theology, he makes little effort to relate it to the opposite point of view that is being loudly expressed by the radical theologians. Lores believes that there is a "high degree of theological homogeneity in the Latin American churches," and he does not desire to risk giving preference to the evangelistic task of the church by entering into "Byzantine arguments."[48]

The one notable occasion when a representative of the Evangelism in Depth point of view squared off against the opposition produced a debate that is still a point of reference in many theological discussions in Latin America.

The April, 1964, issue of *International Review of Missions* carried an initial article by Kenneth Strachan on the Evangelism in Depth program that was largely a description of the process in which the whole concept and method developed. Victor Hayward of the Division of World Mission and Evangelism of the World Council of Churches followed it by a strong criticism, raising questions concerning Strachan's theological position. Hayward's criticism was written from the point of view of the radical, secular theology that we have investigated in earlier chapters. He questions, for example, "the election to salvation of only a small minority of souls"[49] and "God's choosing of privileged favourites."[50] He suggests that we do not "tell men only of a personal salvation offered to those who have faith" but rather "we declare to them that in Christ God has already performed a mighty act to win back this fallen world into the joy of His purposes."[51] He considers as the fundamental question: "Is the correlate of the Gospel the world or the Church?"[52]

Strachan's answer to Hayward, published in the same issue, has contributed "not only a sharper focus on theological presuppositions, but also a more theologically adequate articulation of principles."[53] As Strachan's successor, Horace Fenton, commented concerning the debate: "What is at issue here is not a superficial divergence of opinion, but a profound difference, with far-reaching implications."[54] The Strachan-Hayward exchange is without doubt one of the most significant reference points of the theology of mission and evangelism in our time. A Spanish version has been reprinted in full in *Cuadernos Teológicos*[55] (April-September, 1965).

Strachan answers Hayward's "fundamental issue" by pointing out that it reflects a "false dichotomy between the world and the Church."[56] Strachan refuses to choose between the church or the world as the correlate of the Gospel. He sets forth an alternative point of view:

> Must we not recognize that, regardless of failures in its attitudes or conduct, the Church of the present age *is* in the world, and that the Gospel has been entrusted *to* it *for* the world? So that the Gospel is not a correlate of either the Church or the world, but rather relates through the Church *to* the world.[57]

Strachan is concerned that Hayward, in his concept of God's redemptive purpose in the world, might "overlook or minimize the conditions of repentance and regeneration." Hayward's statement that "the scope of Christ's redemption is as universal as the total life of man" raises serious questions in Strachan's mind. If by this he means, Strachan says, that "God's ultimate triumph is affirmed by conveniently overlooking the demands of God which result in conflict, judgment, and punishment, then there is indeed a basic difference of conviction."[58] Fenton picks up this point and develops it further:

> If Mr. Hayward means, as do so many in the ecumenical camp today (who also deny that they are Universalists), that these men are already being redeemed — the only tragedy being that they do not yet know it — we must take violent exception.[59]

It will be seen that the issue here is similar to that of the "incipient universalism" which has been shown to be present in the theology of some of the representatives of the Latin American radical left.

Another important point that Strachan makes is that the Gospel must be addressed to individuals, not to "the world" or to "men in their social and corporate structures of existence." Strachan asks how Hayward could suggest that the Gospel be "addressed to mankind section by section" in view of "the apostolic pattern of witness directed to the individual in the midst of his family, the household, the community, or the multitude, but ever to him as an individual?"[60]

Emilio Castro, in a subsequent article in the *International Review of Missions,* shows what is probably more of a misunderstanding than outright opposition to Evangelism in Depth by writing:

> If all the members of the Church in Latin America were to devote themselves to a conscious programme for the spread of Christianity on the exhaustive lines of Evangelism in Depth, it would be a tragedy for the Gospel in Latin America; for we should then be taking our members away from their places of responsible witness in society. And while we might add many to our numbers, we should turn many others away, for they would be able to see the Church only as a body wrapped up in itself and irresponsible in the face of the problems of the community.[61]

Here is another false dichotomy. Christians do not need to choose between the Strachan theorem of mobilization of believers for evangelism and the Castro theorem of church members taking responsible places in society. An active and well-adjusted Christian is constantly participating in both simultaneously.

Latin America Mission's Juan Isaís would take exception with Castro that in Evangelism in Depth the church is "wrapped up in itself." In fact he argues effectively that Evangelism in Depth can transform a "centripetal" church into a "centrifugal" church. He says:

> Conceived as a centrifugal movement, Evangelism in Depth is a social event whose cause and origin are in God, but based on the active participation of believers ... the *interior* depth of Evangelism in Depth cannot be considered apart from the culture of the country where this philosophy is carried out in the form of a program.[62]

The active role of the church is a key emphasis in the theologians associated with Evangelism in Depth and the Latin America Mission. John Stam says, "The Church is the divine instrument for the evangelization of the world . . . the Church is the provision of God for the feeding and strengthening of each believer."[63] As believers are built up, they in turn move out centrifugally to win others. Dayton Roberts develops this view of the church further:

> The Church was envisioned as being the family in which new believers are nurtured, the cross section of the body of Christ is to be their spiritual home, the group within which their inner life and evangelistic outreach are to be encouraged, vitalized, and directed.[64]

Roberts believes that evangelicals must change the church structure from a "come" to a "go" structure. "The Church needs a revolution!" he says. By this he means that

> Instead of serving as a corral into which unbelievers must somehow be enticed or driven, it must become a center from which the people and the message go out to touch every needy area of the community and of the world. No other pattern is scriptural. Christians are supposed to be the "salt of the earth." But the salt is stockpiled! The Church has become a warehouse. Let it serve rather as a salt refinery, sending its product into a needy world.[65]

Perhaps this is what Stam had in mind when he wrote that if the theology of Evangelism in Depth provides any new insights they are "within one chapter of the theological encyclopedia, that of ecclesiology."[66] This, of course, is the central issue of theological debate in Latin American Protestantism today.

NOTES TO CHAPTER 5

1. Christian Lalive, *El refugio de las masas: estudio sociológico del protestantismo chileno* (1968), p. 105.

2. John Sinclair, ed., *Protestantism in Latin America: A Bibliographical Guide* (1967).

3. Fernando Vangioni, "Recovering the Apostolic Dynamic," *One Race, One Gospel, One Task*, Carl F. H. Henry and Stanley Mooneyham, eds., I (1967), 150.

4. *Ibid.*, p. 144.

5. *Ibid.*, p. 146.

6. Efraín Santiago, "A Time for Action," *One Race, One Gospel, One Task* (1967), p. 484.

7. Vangioni, *op. cit.*, p. 147.

8. *Ibid.*, p. 149.

9. *Ibid.*, p. 148.

10. *Ibid.*

11. *Ibid.*, p. 149.

12. *Ibid.*, p. 150.

13. Washington Padilla, "No solo de pan vivirá el hombre," *Certeza*, 6, 21 (octubre-diciembre, 1964), p. 31.

14. *Ibid.*, p. 30.

15. *Ibid.*, p. 31.

16. *Ibid.*

17. Washington Padilla, "Jesucristo y los problemas sociales," *Certeza*, 2, 5 (abril-junio, 1960), p. 36.

18. *Ibid.*

19. *Ibid.*

20. Padilla, "No solo de pan vivirá el hombre," p. 32.

21. Padilla, "Jesucristo y los problemas sociales," p. 37.

22. *Ibid.*

23. José María Rico, *Comenzó la vida* (1957). See also in English, *Life Begins for a Jesuit Priest*, by Verne D. Roberts.

24. José María Rico, "Evangelism by Groups," *One Race, One Gospel, One Task*, II (1967), 494.

25. José María Rico, "¿Qué pensar del llamado 'evangelio social'?", *Poder*, No. 109 (1968), p. 15.

26. Rico, "Evangelism by Groups," p. 494.

27. *Ibid.*

28. *Ibid.*

29. Rico, "¿Qué pensar del llamado 'evangelio social'?", p. 14.

30. *Ibid.*

31. *Ibid.*, p. 15.

32. *Ibid.*

33. José D. Fajardo, "The Social Program of the Church," *One Race, One Gospel, One Task*, II, 499.

34. *Ibid.*

35. *Ibid.*

36. *Ibid.*

37. *Ibid.*

38. *Ibid.*

39. *Ibid.*, p. 501.

40. Dayton Roberts, *Revolution in Evangelism: The Story of Evangelism in Depth in Latin America* (1967).

41. John Stam, "Evangelismo a Fondo como revolución teológica," *En Marcha Internacional*, pp. 4-6.

42. Roberts, *op. cit.*, p. 79.

43. Stam, *op. cit.*, p. 4.

44. Kenneth Strachan, "Call to Witness," *International Review of Missions*, LIII, 210 (April, 1964), p. 204.

45. *Ibid.*, p. 205.

46. *Ibid.*, p. 208.

47. *Ibid.*, p. 201.

48. Roberts, *op. cit.*, p. 79.

49. Horace Fenton, "What Is Our Message?" *Latin American Evangelist* (March-April, 1965), p. 1.

50. April-September, 1965.
51. Strachan, *op. cit.*, p. 209.
52. *Ibid.*, p. 210.
53. *Ibid.*, p. 211.
54. Fenton, *op. cit.*, p. 2.
55. Strachan, *op. cit.*, pp. 213-214.
56. Emilio Castro, "Evangelization in Latin America," *International Review of Missions,* LIII, 212 (Oct., 1964), p. 455.
57. Roberts, *op. cit.*, p. 34.
58. Juan Isaís, "Personal Reflections on Evangelism in Depth," p. 3.
59. Stam, *op. cit.*, p. 5.
60. Strachan, *op. cit.*, pp. 213-214.
61. Emilio Castro, "Evangelization in Latin America," p. 455.
62. Juan Isaís, "Personal Reflections on Evangelism in Depth," p. 3.
63. Stam, *op. cit.*, p. 5.
64. Roberts, *op. cit.*, p. 53.
65. *Ibid.*, p. 105.
66. Stam, *op. cit.*, p. 4.

Chapter 6

AN EVANGELICAL VIEW OF SOCIAL SERVICE

Paul Abrecht of the World Council of Churches' Department of Church and Society says in reference to the younger churches, "The most serious obstacle for the Church in meeting the challenge of social change is theological conservatism."[1] The radical theologians in Latin America consistently criticize conservative evangelicals for a lack of social vision.

In all honesty, it must be admitted that there is good reason for this criticism. The sociological study made of Mexican Protestants by William Wonderly and Jorge Lara Braud previously mentioned, indicates quite conclusively that evangelicals tend to form an un-Biblical dichotomy between the church and the world,[2] reaching at times an almost total indifference toward the world in which they live. This study, along with other observations, caused Wonderly to sum up the matter in these words:

> Elsewhere in the spectrum of Latin American Protestantism, and more generally characteristic of it, is the traditional conservative or fundamentalist approach which focuses upon personal salvation of the individual and presents the ideal of separation from the world as a means of a holy life . . . . Conservatives in Latin America have leaned over backwards in the opposite direction, deliberately avoiding involvement in public problems of a social and political nature. They tend to consider evangelism — in its narrow or "spiritual" sense — the only legitimate activity of the Church, and to be wary of current trends toward getting the Church involved in the world.[3]

Christian Lalive, in a recent study, claims that the Chilean Pentecostals are on a "social strike," so completely have they withdrawn from the world.[4]

These criticisms might be slightly exaggerated, such as Wonderly's saying that the *only legitimate* activity of the church in the world is evangelism, according to the evangelicals. Most evangelicals who have given thought to the matter might agree that evangelism is the *top-priority* activity, but not the only legitimate one. Still the general feeling that evangelicals have been dragging their feet in social matters is in the main an accurate one.

Not that the ability to criticize evangelicals means that the radical and secular theologians who have specialized in social ethics have necessarily come to the right conclusions. Their consultations, encounters, reports, magazines, research projects, social experiments, and other activities at times have taken them to something less than acceptable conclusions. One wonders whether God ever intended that the church be sufficiently competent to pass judgment on such complex social issues as are being commented upon in the left-wing journals. Wonderly criticizes the ISAL group, for example, for having their heads too far in the clouds. "One gets the impression," he says, "that their concern tends to be focused more on the higher levels of national and international politics than on a social action based on the kind of concrete investigation that Hopper calls 'the toilsome business of research among real people and on real problems.' "[5] Wonderly feels that the ISAL commitment to violent revolution "appears to call for a premature capitulation and abdication of responsibility on the part of the church."[6] The serious danger of ISAL's approach is "committing the Church to action on the basis of decisions made either without sufficient use of the insights of empirical research or through an uncritical and eclectic use of them, influenced partly by emotional and nationalistic factors."[7]

As qualified an expert as John Mackay sees the positive dimension of the approach that the evangelical wing of the church takes toward social issues. He says,

> As to the Protestant churches in Latin America in relation to the new revolutionary mood, the picture is spotty. The "non-historical" churches, in particular the Pentecostal, are closer to the realities of the human situation today and are confronting the revolutionary social crisis with more understanding than one finds in general among the missions and churches of the major Protestant denominations.[8]

Mackay sees the Pentecostals as true "spiritual revolutionaries." They have taken a strong position with regard to their relationship with the world, yet they have "an answer for the deep yearnings of the common people."[9]

Within the past decade, evangelical leaders have become increasingly aware of their weaknesses in the area of social ethics, and have expressed a desire to overcome them. Horace Fenton admits that "many evangelicals reacted violently to the social gospel of the early twentieth century and proclaimed instead a message that had no social dimension whatever."[10] Wilton Nelson of the Latin American Bible Seminary says:

> The man who has Christ in his heart should be very sensitive to the suffering and the need of the world that surrounds him. Consequently, if a man calls himself a Christian, and shows no social concern, something is quite evidently wrong with his Christianity.[11]

It may safely be said that virtually all Latin American Protestants are concerned with the social witness of the church. There are, however, some areas of disagreement as to the implications of this witness as far as the church is concerned. The crucial problem areas include:

(1) Some, such as Emilio Castro, believe that we should concentrate on changing society so that we will ultimately enjoy more success in preaching the Gospel. He says, "The society which we should aim for is that in which man can respond freely and responsibly to the preaching of the Word of God."[12] This, however, sounds somewhat utopian, and at the same time a reversal of the order that "you shall know the Truth and the Truth shall make you free" (John 8:32). Still, it is a commonly held goal of social action.

(2) Some believe that the church should aim to become so involved in the world that it ceases to exist as an institution. This, of course, is an extreme viewpoint which few other than certain intellectual elites would agree upon.

(3) One of the more typical evangelical problems is that raised by José María Rico as to whether the church should use its resources directly in attempting to change society at all, or whether all resources should be employed in changing men so that they in turn will change society. This might be called the indirect approach to social service.

(4) The question of whether social service is an end in itself or a means to another end (e.g., winning souls) is anoth-

er problem that must be studied by evangelicals in more detail.

The crucial issue, then, is not so much whether the church should have a social concern or not — all agree that it should. The issue is how to balance the evangelistic, soul-saving ministry over against the social activities of the church. The following section will be an attempt to set forth one evangelical point of view that hopefully progresses toward the answers to some of these questions.

The relationship of the church to the world could include a long list of many good things for the church to do. We are not here interested in such a list, however, unless some scale of priorities can be developed along with it. In order to set forth a coherent strategy of missions and evangelism, and in order properly to invest the resources of the church, priorities must be determined. Therefore we will first set forth the *primary* relationship of the church to the world, followed by the *secondary* relationship.

The Primary Relationship of the Church to the World

In order to determine this relationship, we first of all should describe how things presently stand. The Bible teaches that the most prominent characteristic of the mutual involvement of the church and the world is antagonism. The church in essence is a special group of *people.* The same holds true for the world. We are dealing, then, with two collective human factions, and these factions are in conflict. The church is "the household of God" (Eph. 2:19), a family of people who have been reconciled to God through Christ and have placed themselves under His lordship. Numerically they constitute a minority of the human race. According to 1 John 5:19 they are "of God" while the rest of the human race makes up "the whole world," which lies "in the power of the evil one." The people of the world are descendants of the first Adam and are material, earthy, natural. Those of the church have been born again and are descendants of the last Adam, spiritual, heavenly (1 Cor. 15:42-50). Those who have not been born the second time into Christ, and who do not form a part of His body, the church (1 Cor. 12), "cannot inherit the kingdom of God." These two families of human beings are clearly distinguished as "the children of God" and "the children of the devil" in 1 John 3:10.

The Kingdom of God is basically an eschatological event in the New Testament, and the church awaits "the age to come" with great anticipation. It will not arrive before Christ's second coming (Matt. 24:3). In the meantime we all live in "this present age," which the Bible characterizes as an "evil age" and "something to be delivered from" (Gal. 1:4). The powers of this age battle against the powers of the age to come. The "God of this age" is Satan himself, who "hath blinded the minds of them that believe not, lest the light of the glorious Gospel should shine unto them" (2 Cor. 4:4). Since Satan is its god, in a sense this world can be considered the kingdom of the devil, as Jesus Himself calls it in Luke 11:18. This is why Satan could offer it all to Christ at His temptation (Matt. 4:8-9). Christ rejected the temptation, but did not deny the validity of the offer.

The Kingdom of God, or the age to come, has invaded today's world in a real but anticipatory way. Christ's death on the cross sealed the doom of Satan (Heb. 2:14), but he is still permitted great power in his world (1 Pet. 5:8). The preliminary manifestation of the Kingdom of God is intimately related to the church. In Matthew 16, Christ promises Peter that He will build His church, and as part of this process He will provide the "keys to the kingdom of heaven." While the church as a social institution is not to be identified completely with the Kingdom of God, still the power of God manifested in this present age is manifested through the instrumentality of the true body of Christ, the church.

This distinction between the two kingdoms is extremely important in today's tension with secular theology, since it is one of the Biblical teachings that has been quite generally de-emphasized by those of the radical left. While some evangelical dispensationalists might not be in total agreement with the above reasoning, all evangelicals recognize the power of Satan in the world today, and the essential conflict between the church and the world. There is no need to deny that this describes a dualism. Naturally it is not an eternal, metaphysical dualism in the Greek sense, since God is and always has been sovereign. But in the mysterious plan of God for this world, He obviously permits a temporal dualism, and desires that His children be involved in some way in "this present evil age."

What kind of involvement does God desire? Christians are "to marvel not that the world hates you" (1 John 3:13). They are to "love not the world, neither the things of the world" (1 John 2:15). They are to enter the conflict and "overcome the world" (1 John 5:4). This is the negative dimension.

The positive dimension of the Christian's involvement in the world is found in our Lord's high-priestly prayer in John 17. He uses the term "world" nineteen times. While it is true that believers have been taken "out of the world" (v. 6), Christ in turn sends them "into the world" (v. 18). While they are in the world, they are not to be "of the world" (v. 14) since the "world hates them" (v. 14). The principal objective of sending believers into the world is "that the world might believe" (v. 21).

Once the church has gone into the world, its principal responsibility there is to preach the Gospel. God desires that multitudes be reconciled to Himself. He is "not willing that any should perish, but that all should come to repentance" (2 Pet. 3:9). In order to bring this about, God has chosen as His instrument a body of Christians preaching the Gospel, referred to in today's theological terminology as the kerygma. Faith can only come to an individual "by hearing," and hearing "by the Word of God" (Rom. 10:17). In order to believe, those of the world must hear, in order to hear there must be a preacher, and in order to preach they must be sent (Rom. 10: 14-15). The church is in the world, then, for the *primary* (but not exclusive) purpose of announcing the kerygma.

But even the announcement of the kerygma is only a means to another end. The objective, according to the Great Commission, is to "make disciples" and "baptize them," which indicates that they should become members of the church (Matt. 29:19). When they come out of the world through the persuasion of those who are already disciples of Christ, and into the church, they enjoy the Christian fellowship called koinonia. In this intimate fellowship of the "household of God" they "come together" (1 Cor. 11:17) to be "perfected" and "edified" (Eph. 4:12). But koinonia should never be an end in itself either, and this has been one area of weakness in some of the evangelical churches in Latin America. If a church makes it an end, Juan Isaís would call it a "centripetal" church. Koinonia serves to prepare believers to take their places in the centrifugal movement of kerygma.

It is somewhat disturbing to evangelicals when such theologians as Davies call this obviously Biblical teaching "ecclesiolatry."[13] This is not worshipping the church; it is

105

loving the world as "God so loved the world" (John 3:16). What greater love could Christians show to the world than announcing the kerygma and persuading them to be reconciled to God (2 Cor. 11:20)?

The Secondary Relationship of the Church to the World

The reconciliation of multitudes of men and women to God through Christ is the *primary* relationship of the church to the world. There is also a *secondary relationship*, which we have already defined as social service, called diakonia. Christian social service embraces all the good works that the church is capable of performing in the world. It is a necessary outcome of the new birth. "Faith without works is dead." Jesus taught that Christians are the "salt of the earth" and the "light of the world." This involves public service in which men may "see your good works and glorify your Father who is in heaven" (Matt. 5:16).

When Jesus told the lawyer that he must "love his neighbor as himself," the lawyer requested a more detailed definition of "neighbor." Jesus followed with the parable of the good Samaritan (Luke 10:25-37). To help the needy with no thought of personal benefit is a Christian responsibility and pleases God. Therefore, whether a Christian relates to social needs is not optional.

There is, however, a scriptural priority as to which social needs to take care of first. A Christian is first and foremost responsible for his own family, in whatever manner his particular culture might define what "family" means. "If any provide not for his own, and specially for those of his own house, he hath denied the faith, and is worse than an infidel" (1 Tim. 5:8). Breadwinning is the first step in Christian diakonia.

The second step is provision for the needs of those of the wider spiritual family of the church. The Bible, in relating the total social ministry of the church to a more particular aspect, says, "As we have opportunity, let us do good unto all men, especially unto them who are of the household of faith" (Gal. 6:10). The early church set an example for us in this respect by "having all things common ... parting to all men as every man had need" (Acts 2:44-45). First-century economic solutions might not be transferable to the twentieth century, but the principle of caring for the social needs of fellow believers is most important. It seems that the implication here is that when resources for social service are limited, all other things being equal, the needs of fellow believers must be met before those of society in general.

The parable of the good Samaritan teaches us that social service must not be limited to either the immediate family or the household of God. One reason the Samaritan was good was that he helped the wounded man in spite of his being of another faith and another ethnic group. Christian social service must reach out into the "world" and exhibit the diakonia that the new birth demands.

But, if the church is going to reach out into the world with social service, what should be the motives? We have already seen that it is the desire of God, and hopefully the church, to win the maximum number of men and women to Christ. But the question here is whether social service should be considered primarily as a *means toward that end*, or perhaps as an *end in itself*. In other words, how can we measure the success or failure of diakonia? Obviously we measure success of evangelism in terms of how many disciples are made and baptized into the church. Do we measure diakonia the same way? Or do we measure the success of diakonia in terms of to what degree the social and material needs of people are alleviated through our efforts?

When the church moves into the world with the kerygma or preaching of the Gospel, many secondary means are used toward the end of persuading people to be reconciled to God. Evangelistic campaigns, personal contacts, visitation programs, mass media, missionary societies, modern transportation — all can be utilized in the effort. Should diakonia be added to this list?

It seems that, biblically speaking, loving one's neighbor should not be considered as a means to an end. Love carries no price tag. True love does not say, "I will love you *if*..." Christ's success in curing the ten lepers was not measured by how many came back, although the one who did was a cause of great rejoicing. His act of mercy was successful because all ten lepers were cured. Nevertheless, faith *can* result from diakonia. The good Samaritan did not say, "I'll pay your hotel bill *if*..." José Fajardo would call that the banana-halter approach, and he feels that it should not be at the root of the Christian social service program. When missionaries to China distributed food only to those who would come to their church, they inadvertently added a new term to the English language: "rice Christians."

We do not intend to discuss the methods that the church should use when it moves into the world with diakonia. These are optional. They may involve capitalism or they may involve socialism. They may imply gradual evolution or violent revolution. They may involve building a home for the aged or agitating for a new social security law. They will certainly vary from one country to another and perhaps from one subculture to another within the same country. If Christians are to carry out their social responsibility in the world they are obligated to become informed as to how the social needs of their country may best be met, and then proceed to meet them. But since human opinion varies greatly as to solutions for today's complex socio-economic-political problems, complete freedom should be granted to individuals.

In spite of the fact that Christian social service may be considered as an end in itself, whatever opportunities it presents for a positive Christian and evangelistic testimony should not be lost. Those who receive Christian social aid should receive it in "the name of the Lord" (Mark 9:41). The Christian's "light of the world" should never be hid under a bushel. Diakonia is distinguished from philanthropy, not necessarily by technical or material factors, but rather by the public knowledge that it is done "in the name of the Lord."

Much of the criticism of the radical left against the evangelical wing of the church in Latin America concerning its secondary relationship to the world through diakonia is well taken. Evangelicals, however, have begun to awaken to this responsibility, and it is hoped that the process will contine accelerating. As long as the secondary does not begin to take the place of the primary, this will be pleasing to God.

NOTES TO CHAPTER 6

1. Paul Abrecht, *The Churches and Rapid Social Change* (1961), p. 48.
2. William Wonderly and Jorge Lara Braud, *Los evangélicos somos así* (1964).
3. William Wonderly, "Social Science Research and the Church in Latin America," *Practical Anthropology*, 14, 4 (July-August, 1967), p. 170.
4. Christian Lalive, *El refugio de las masas: estudio sociológico del protestantismo chileno* (1968), pp. 163ff.
5. Wonderly, *op. cit.*, p. 166.
6. *Ibid.*, p. 167.
7. *Ibid.*

8. John Mackay, "Latin America and Revolution," *Christian Century,* LXXXII, 46, and LXXXII, 47, p. 1441.

9. *Ibid.*, p. 1439.

10. Horace Fenton, "Mission and Social Concern," *His* Magazine (February, 1968), p. 15.

11. Wilton Nelson, "The Unworldly and Worldly Character of the Gospel," *Latin American Evangelist* (September-October, 1968), p. 9.

12. Emilio Castro, "Prólogo," *Comunidad civil y comunidad cristiana* (1967), p. 25.

13. J. G. Davies, *Diálogo con el mundo* (1967).

BIBLIOGRAPHY

ABRECHT, Paul. *The Churches and Rapid Social Change.* New York, Doubleday, 1961.

ALVEZ, Rubem. "El ministerio social de la iglesia local," *Responsabilidad social del cristiano.* Montevideo, ISAL, 1964, pp. 56-66.

"Injusticia y rebelión," *Cristianismo y Sociedad*, Año II, No. 6, 1964, Montevideo, Junta Latinoamericana de Iglesia y Sociedad, pp. 40-53.

BAEZ CAMARGO, Gonzálo. "Mexico — a Long Stretch from Edinburgh," *Ecumenical Review*, XVI:3, April, 1964, pp. 266-278.

BARREIRO, Julio. "La naturaleza del hombre en Marx," *Hombre, Ideología y Revolución en América Latina.* Montevideo, ISAL, 1965, pp. 19-41.

BEATO, Joaquín. "La misión profética de la iglesia evangélica en América Latina," *La naturaleza de la iglesia y su misión en Latinoamérica.* Bogotá, CCPAL, 1963.

"Ideología Cristá como base para a acao social de Igreja," *Cristianismo y Sociedad*, I:1. Montevideo, ISAL, 1963, pp. 9-20.

BERGER, Peter L. "A Sociological View of the Secularization of Theology," *Journal for the Scientific Study of Religion*, Spring, 1967, pp. 3-16.

BISHOP, Jordan, O.P. "Numerical Growth — an Adequate Criterion of Mission?" *International Review of Missions*, LVII:227, July, 1968, pp. 248-290.

BUCAFUSCO, Luis P. *Laicos Activos: Iglesia Viva.* Buenos Aires, La Aurora, 1955.

CASTILLO CARDENAS, Gonzálo. "El desafío de la América Latina a las iglesias evangélicas," *La naturaleza de la iglesia y su misión en Latinoamérica.* Bogotá, CCPAL, 1963, pp. 38-51.

"Protestant Christianity in Latin America," *Student World*, 57:1, 1964, pp. 61-66.

"The Life and Witness of the Church in Latin America," *Witness in Six Continents.* London, Edinburgh House Press, 1964, pp. 29-36.

"Christians and the Struggle for a New Social Order in Latin America," mimeographed. Address to World Conference on Church and Society, Geneva, 1966.

"Los cristianos y la lucha por un nuevo orden social en América Latina," *Cristianismo y Sociedad*, IV:12. Montevideo, ISAL, 1966, pp. 84-96.

CASTRO, Emilio. *"Cuando molesta la conciencia . . . "* Buenos Aires, La Aurora, 1962.

"Nuestra tarea inconclusa," *Cristo, la esperanza para América Latina.* Buenos Aires, Confederación Evangélica del Río de la Plata, 1962, pp. 92-110.

"Christian Response to the Latin American Revolution," *Christianity and Crisis,* 23, 15, 1963, pp. 160-163.

Misión, presencia y diálogo. Buenos Aires, Methopress, 1964.

"Evangelization in Latin America," *International Review of Missions,* LIII:212, October, 1964, pp. 452-456.

"Bible and Church in Latin America," *Bulletin of the United Bible Societies,* 2-3 Quarters, 1964, pp. 78-84.

"En busca de la estructura misionera de la congregación," *Cuadernos Teológicos,* XIII:3, 1964, pp. 83-86.

"Posibilidad de la fe en los países socialistas," *El Predicador Evangélico,* XXII:88, 1965, Buenos Aires, La Aurora, pp. 248-253.

"The Perspective of the Cross," *Study Encounter,* 3:3. Message to WCC Conference on Church and Society, Geneva, 1966, pp. 106-108.

"Protestants in the Latin American Revolution," paper presented in Bogotá, Oct., 1966.

"Misión y evangelización," *Id por el mundo.* Buenos Aires, Methopress, 1966, pp. 15-29.

"Conversión y transformación social," ponencia mimeografiada para la Consulta Continental de Evangelismo, Cochabamba, junio-julio, 1966. Iglesia Metodista.

"How the Church Contributes to the Transformation of Society," *World Christian Education,* second and third quarters. Report from WCC Conference on Church and Society, Geneva, 1966, pp. 47-48.

"Prólogo," *Comunidad civil y comunidad cristiana,* por Karl Barth. Montevideo, Ediciones Tauro (ULAJE), 1967, pp. 7-28.

"Evangelism and Social Justice," *The Ecumenical Review,* XX:2, 1968, Geneva, WCC, pp. 146-150.

C.C.P.A.L. *La naturaleza de la iglesia y su misión en Latinoamérica:* Materiales preparatorios, ponencias y conclusiones del Congreso de Estudio sobre "La naturaleza de la iglesia y su misión en Latinoamérica hoy," 1-8 de diciembre de 1963. Bogotá, Iqueima.

111

CESAR, Waldo A. "The Church's Task in Politics," Ch. 5 of *Raise the Signal*, H. S. Converse, ed. New York, Friendship, 1961.

CHARTIER, Ricardo A. "Modos de la relación entre la iglesia y la sociedad, *Cristianismo y Sociedad*, Año I, No. 2, 1963, Montevideo, Junta Latinoamericana de Iglesia y Sociedad, pp. 5-13.

"Relaciones entre la iglesia y la sociedad," *Responsabilidad social del cristiano*. Montevideo, ISAL, 1964, pp. 45-55.

"La iglesia en una sociedad en transformación," *Id por el mundo*. Buenos Aires, Methopress, 1966, pp. 60-84.

"Saul Alinsky: el conflicto y la controversia en la organización de la comunidad," *Cristianismo y Sociedad*, V:14. Montevideo, ISAL, 1967, pp. 103-111.

CHARTIER, E. A., NIILUS, L., y SABANES, C. M. "Missionary Structures and Training for Mission — The River Plate Area," *International Review of Missions*, LVII:226, April, 1968. Geneva, WCC, pp. 217-228.

CONFEDERACION EVANGELICA DEL RIO DE LA PLATA. *Cristo, La Esperanza de la América Latina:* Ponencias, Informes, Comentarios de la segunda conferencia evangélica latinoamericana, 20 de julio a 6 de agosto de 1961, Lima, Perú. Buenos Aires.

CONTERIS, Hiber. "El marco ideológico de la revolución latinoamericana," *Cristianismo y Sociedad*, II:5, 1964, Montevideo, ISAL, pp. 36-51.

"El rol de la Iglesia en el cambio social de América Latina," *Cristianismo y Sociedad*, III:7, 1965, Montevideo, ISAL, pp. 53-60.

CONTERIS, Hiber, ed. *Fe cristiana y marxismo*. Montevideo, ISAL, 1965.

Hombre, Ideología y Revolución en América Latina. Montevideo, ISAL, 1965.

CONVERSE, Hyla Stuntz, ed. *Raise the Signal*. New York, Friendship Press, 1961.

COX, Harvey. *The Secular City*. New York, Macmillan, 1965.

CRISTIANISMO Y SOCIEDAD. "II Consulta Latinoamericana de Iglesia y Sociedad," *Cristianismo y Sociedad*, Número Doble, Año III, No. 9 y Año IV, No. 10, 1966, Montevideo, Junta Latinoamericana de Iglesia y Sociedad, pp. 83-102.

DAVIES, J. G. *Diálogo con el mundo*. Buenos Aires, Methopress, 1967.

"Church Growth: A Critique," *International Review of Missions*, LVII:227, July, 1968. Geneva, WCC, pp. 291-297.

DEBRAY, Régis. *Revolution in the Revolution? Armed Struggle and Political Struggle in Latin America.* New York, Monthly Review Press, 1967.

ESCOBAR, Samuel. "Diálogo entre Cristo y Marx," *Certeza,* 7:25, enero-marzo, 1966, pp. 4-8.

FAJARDO, José D. "The Social Program of the Church," *One Race, One Gospel, One Task,* Vol. II. Minneapolis, Worldwide Publications, 1967, pp. 498-501.

FENTON, Horace L. "What Is Our Message?" *Latin American Evangelist,* March-April, 1965, pp. 1-4.

"Mission and Social Concern," *His* Magazine, February, 1968, pp. 14-16.

FRANCO, Pablo. "La influencia de los Estados Unidos en América Latina," *Cristianismo y Sociedad,* V:13, 1967, Montevideo, ISAL.

GALLAND, Valdo. "God's Present Work in Latin America," Ch. 1 of *Raise the Signal,* H. S. Converse, ed. New York, Friendship, 1961.

GARNER, William R. "The Sino-Soviet Ideological Struggle in Latin America," *Journal of Inter-American Studies,* X:2, April, 1968, pp. 244-255.

GONZALEZ, Justo L. *Revolución y encarnación.* Río Piedras, Librería "La Reforma," 1965.

Por la renovación del entendimiento, la educación teológica en la América Latina. Río Piedras, Librería "La Reforma," 1965.

GREEN, Dana. "Ecumenical Perspectives in Promoting Justice and Peace in Latin America," address presented to the Inaugural Conference of the Institute of World Justice and Peace, Catholic University of Puerto Rico, March 31, 1967.

HOUTART, Francois, and PIN, Emile. *The Church and the Latin American Revolution.* New York, Sheed and Ward, 1965.

IGLESIA Y SOCIEDAD EN AMERICA LATINA. *Encuentro y Desafío,* Conclusiones y resoluciones de la Primera Consulta Evangélica Latinoamericana sobre Iglesia y Sociedad realizada en Huampaní, Perú, del 23 al 27 de julio de 1961. Montevideo, ISAL.

La responsabilidad social del cristiano. guia de estudios. Montevideo, ISAL, 1964.

América Hoy, acción de Dios y responsabilidad del hombre. Montevideo, ISAL, 1966.

"Un intento de 'encarnación,' " *Cristianismo y Sociedad,* V:14. Montevideo, ISAL, 1966, pp. 113-119.

113

ISAIS, Juan M. "Personal Reflections on Evangelism in Depth." Mimeographed, Office of Worldwide Evangelism in Depth, Latin America Mission, Bogota, N.J., Latin America Mission, 1968.

LALIVE D'EPINAY, Christian. "The Pentecostal 'Conquista' in Chile," *The Ecumenical Review*, XX:1, January, 1968, pp. 16-32.

El refugio de las masas: estudio sociológico del protestantismo chileno. Santiago de Chile, Editorial del Pacífico, 1968.

LARA BRAUD, Jorge. "Revolution in the Western Hemisphere," an address given at the annual meeting of Methodists of the Southern Central Region, mimeographed, 10/31/66.

"Latin America's Challenge to the Church — the Issues We Face," mimeographed, 11/16/66.

"Protestants and the Process of Integration," *Integration of Man and Society in Latin America*, Samuel Shapiro, ed., Notre Dame, University of Notre Dame Press, 1967, pp. 209-214.

LATHAM, Robert O. *God For All Men, The Meeting of the Commission on World Mission and Evangelism of the World Council of Churches at Mexico City, December 8th to 19th, 1963.* London, Edinburgh House Press, 1964.

LIGGETT, Tomas J. "El evangelio y la misión de la iglesia," *La naturaleza de la iglesia y su misión en Latinoamérica*. Bogotá, CCPAL, 1963.

LINDSELL, Harold, ed. *The Church's Worldwide Mission.* Waco, Texas, Word Books, 1966.

"Attack Syncretism with Dialogue," *Evangelical Missions Quarterly*, 3:4, Summer, 1967, pp. 203-208.

"Uppsala 1968," *Christianity Today*, August 16, 1968, p. 6.

LLOREDA, Alfonso. "Prophetic Vision in the Evangelistic Expression of the Protestant Church in Latin America," *Witness in Six Continents.* London, Edinburgh House Press, 1964.

"Y la Biblia llegó hasta los otomíes," *Certeza*, julio-septiembre, 1964.

LØNNING, Per. "The Theological Basis of the Geneva Conference," *Christian Century*, March 1, 1967, pp. 270-271.

LORES, Rubén. "Algunas reflexiones en torno a los fundamentos teológicos de Evangelismo a fondo," ponencia para la Consulta Continental de Evangelización de la Iglesia Metodista. Cochabamba, Bolivia, 26 de junio al 7 de julio 1966, policopiado. Cochabamba, Bolivia, 8 pp.

"Evangelism in Depth," *One Race, One Gospel, One Task,* Vol. II. Minneapolis, Worldwide, 1967, pp. 495-497.

"The Mission of Missions Today," *Latin America Evangelist,* Sept.-Oct., 1967.

MCGAVRAN, Donald A. "Wrong Strategy: The Real Crisis in Missions," *International Review of Missions,* LIV:216, October, 1965, pp. 451-461.

"Missions: Passive and Active," *The Presbyterian Journal,* Aug. 2, 1967, pp. 9-10.

"Will Uppsala Betray the Two Billion?" *Church Growth Bulletin,* IV:5, May, 1968, pp. 1-6.

"Church Growth Strategy Continued," *International Review of Missions,* LVII:227, July, 1968, pp. 335-343.

Understanding Church Growth. Grand Rapids, Eerdmans, 1969.

MACKAY, John A. "Latin America and Revolution," *Christian Century,* LXXXII:46, pp. 1409-1412. LXXXII:47, 1439-1443, 1965.

MIGUEZ BONINO, José. "Fundamentos bíblicos y teológicos de la responsabilidad social de la iglesia," *Encuentro y Desafío.* Buenos Aires, ISAL, 1961, pp. 19-26.

"Nuestro mensaje," *Cristo la esperanza para América Latina.* Buenos Aires, Confederación Evangélica del Río de la Plata, 1962, pp. 67-91.

"Fundamentos teológicos de la responsabilidad social de la iglesia," *Responsabilidad social del cristiano.* Montevideo, ISAL, 1964, pp. 22-31.

Polémica, diálogo y misión: catolicismo romano y protestantismo en la América Latina. Montevideo, Centro de Estudios Cristianos, 1966.

"Un Dios que actúa y renueva la iglesia," *América Hoy.* Montevideo, ISAL, 1966, pp. 37-55.

"Main Currents of Protestantism," *Integration of Man and Society in Latin America,* Samuel Shapiro, ed. Notre Dame, University of Notre Dame Press, 1967, pp. 191-201.

"Christians and the Political Revolution," *Risk,* Stephen C. Ross, ed., 1967, 1-2. Geneva, WCC, pp. 100-110.

NELSON, Wilton. "The Unworldly and Worldly Character of the Gospel," *Latin American Evangelist,* September-October, 1968, pp. 7-9.

NIELSEN, Ernesto. "Presencia y misión del cristianismo evangélico en la América Latina," *Polémica, Diálogo y Misión,* José Míguez B., ed. Montevideo, Centro de Estudios Cristianos, 1966.

ODELL, Luis E., BOLIOLI, Oscar, FRANCO, Leonardo and CASTRO, Emilio. "How Latin America Sees It," *Christian Century*, LXXXII:25, June 23, 1965, 805-806.

PADILLA, Washington. "Jesucristo y los problemas sociales," *Certeza*, 2:5, abril-junio, 1960, pp. 36-37.

"No solo de pan vivirá el hombre," *Certeza*, 6:21, octubre-diciembre, 1964, pp. 30-33.

PANTELIS, Jorge. "La dimensión evangelista de la iglesia," *Avance*, La Paz, marzo-abril, 1968, pp. 2, 10.

READ, William R., MONTERROSO, Victor M., and JOHNSON, Harmon A. *Latin American Church Growth*. Grand Rapids, Eerdmans, 1969.

RICO, José María. *Comenzó la Vida*, segunda edición. Cochabamba, Imprenta Atlantic, 1957. See also in English, *Life Begins for a Jesuit Priest*, by Verne D. Roberts. Bolivian Indian Mission, n.d., n.p.

"Evangelism by Groups," *One Race, One Gospel, One Task*, Vol. II. Minneapolis, Worldwide, 1967, pp. 492-494.

"¿Qué pensar del llamado 'evangelio social'?" *Poder*, No. 109, 1968, Miami, Editorial Vida, pp. 14-15.

RIOS, Roberto E. "¿Qué estructuras de las congregaciones locales impiden la obra misionera?" *Cuadernos Teológicos*, XIII:3, julio-septiembre, 1964, pp. 87-94.

ROBERTS, W. Dayton. *Revolution in Evangelism: The Story of Evangelism in Depth in Latin America*. Chicago, Moody, 1967.

SANTA ANA, Julio de. "Editorial," *Cristianismo y Sociedad*, Año 1, No. 2, 1963, Montevideo, Junta Latinoamericana de Iglesia y Sociedad, pp. 1-3.

SANTIAGO, Efraín. "A Time for Action," *One Race, One Gospel, One Task*. Minneapolis, Worldwide, 1967, pp. 481-484.

SAPSEZIAN, Aharon. "The Emerging Sense of National Identity," Ch. 6 of *Raise the Signal*, H. S. Converse, ed. New York, Friendship, 1961.

SHAULL, M. Richard. "Evangelism and Proselytism in Latin America," *Student World*. 46:1, 1953, pp. 14-20.

Encounter with Revolution. New York, Association Press, 1955.

"New Forms of Church Life in a New Society," Ch. 7 of *Raise the Signal*, H. S. Converse, ed. New York, Friendship, 1961.

116

"Recientes estudios sobre el desarrollo político en Asia, Africa, y América Latina," *Cristianismo y Sociedad,* Año 1, No. 2, 1963, Montevideo, Junta Latinoamericana de Iglesia y Sociedad, pp. 43-50.

"The New Revolutionary Mood in Latin America," *Christianity and Crisis,* 23:5, 1963, pp. 44-48.

"La iglesia y la situación político-ideológica de América Latina," *La naturaleza de la iglesia y su misión en Latinoamérica.* Bogotá, CCPAL, 1963.

"La forma de la iglesia en la nueva diáspora," *Cristianismo y Sociedad,* Año II, No. 6, 1964, Montevideo, Junta Latinoamericana de Iglesia y Sociedad, pp. 3-17.

"Ideología, fe y revolución social," *Testimonium,* X:2, 1964, Geneva, MEC, pp. 41-47.

"Una perspectiva cristiana del desarrollo histórico y social," *Hombre, ideología y revolución en América Latina.* Montevideo, ISAL,1965, pp. 78-91.

"Hacia una perspectiva cristiana de la revolución social — Nicolás Berdaiev," *Cristianismo y Sociedad,* III:7, 1965, Montevideo, ISAL, pp. 6-16.

"Christian Initiative in Latin American Revolution," *Christianity and Crisis,* XXV:23, January 10, 1966, pp. 295-298.

"The Revolutionary Challenge to Church and Theology," *Princeton Seminary Bulletin,* 60:1, October, 1966, pp. 24-32.

"El cambio revolucionario en una perspectiva teológica," *Cristianismo y Sociedad,* IV:12, 1966, Montevideo, ISAL, pp. 49-70.

"Y un Dios que actúa y transforma la historia," *América Hoy.* Montevideo, ISAL, 1966, pp. 57-70.

"Revolution: Heritage and Contemporary Option," Part Two of *Containment and Change* by Carl Oglesby and Richard Shaull. New York, Macmillan, 1967, pp. 179 248.

"Next Stage in Latin America," *Christianity and Crisis,* Nov. 13, 1967, pp. 264-266.

"The New Latin Revolutionaries and the U.S.," *Christian Century,* LXXXV:3, January 17, 1968, pp. 69-70.

"Toward a Reformation of Objectives," chapter in *Protestant Crosscurrents in Mission, The Ecumenical-Conservative Encounter.* Nashville, Abingdon, 1968.

117

SHEPHERD, Jack F. "Mission — and Syncretism," *The Church's Worldwide Mission*. Waco, Word Books, 1966, pp. 85-95.

SINCLAIR, John H., ed. *Protestantism in Latin America: A Bibliographical Guide*. Austin, Hispanic American Institute, 1967.

STAM, Juan. "Evangelismo a fondo como revolución teológica," *En Marcha Internacional*, 1968, pp. 4-6.

STRACHAN, R. Kenneth. "Call to Witness," *International Review of Missions*, April, 1964, LIII:210, pp. 191-215.

TRON, Juan and CESARI, Antonio. "Evangelización, comunidad y proselytismo," *Polémica, Diálogo y Misión*, José Míguez B., ed. Montevideo, Centro de Estudios Cristianos, 1966, pp. 48-67.

VALLE, Carlos. "Presuposiciones teológicas de la evangelización," ponencia mimeografiada para la Consulta Continental de Evangelización, Cochabamba, 26 de junio-7 de julio. Iglesia Metodista, 1966.

VANGIONI, Fernando. "Recovering the Apostolic Dynamic," *One Race, One Gospel, One Task*, Carl F. H. Henry and Stanley Mooneyham, eds., Vol. 1. Minneapolis, Worldwide, 1967, pp. 142-150.

VISSER 'T HOOFT, W. A. *No Other Name: The Choice Between Syncretism and Christian Universalism*. Philadelphia, Westminster, 1963.

WIPFLER, William L. "A Column Dedicated to Dialogue," *Latin American News Letter*, December, 1967. New York, LAD/DOM/NCC, p. 9.

WONDERLY, William L. "Social Science Research and the Church in Latin America," *Practical Anthropology*, 14:4, July-August 1967, pp. 161-173.

WONDERLY, William L., and LARA BRAUD, Jorge. *Los evangélicos somos así*. Mexico, Comisión Evangélica de Estudios y Comité de Literatura Evangélica, 1964.

DATE DUE

11.13.'85	